# Gift Giving From Him To Her

## What Every Woman Wishes He Knew About Gifts

Co-authors

Rita Rochte and Georgia Meredith

Sunkist House Publishing, Los Altos, California

FIRST EDITION

Copyright 1991

By Rita Rochte and Georgia Meredith

Published in the United States of America

By Sunkist House Publishers, Los Altos, California, 94022

**Library of Congress Catalogue Card Number: 91 - 65817**

**ISBN** 0-9614705-1-8

All the names in our examples are fictitious unless otherwise noted. The stories are based on real life events, in some instances they have been developed from compilations.

Cover Design by Barbara Clark

Celebrities, speakers, and authors often say that they couldn't have done it without -- and then list everyone from their first grade teacher to the newspaper deliverer. Trust us, we could not have done it without these people:

The insightful men and women who let us ask them endless questions and gave us their wonderful stories

Our husbands who gave support and editorial suggestions

Jerry and son Phillip's patient assistance with the devilish computers

Sue Patigalia Shoff and Linda Anderson for their early editing

Alice Holstein for her thoughtful, persistent and speedy editing

R.R. and G.M.

# TABLE OF CONTENTS

**READING SUGGESTION:** It is NOT necessary for you to read this book in the order it is printed. If you have an immediate gift question, feel free to go directly to the appropriate chapter. Please come back later.

# A Few Words to Women

You bought this book for the man in your life for a reason. You are hoping it will help him learn how to give you gifts you would love to receive. You want this book to give him lessons in the "magic" of gifts. No more electrical appliances on anniversaries.

That is exactly what the first three-fourths of the book will do.

However, gift giving does not occur in a vacuum - there is a giver AND a receiver. That is why the final portion of this book is directed to you — what you as women need to know to make the whole process successful.

We do recommend that you read the part called *For Her* before you give the book to him.

# The Gift Problem

*The hardest thing for a man to do is buy a gift for a woman, especially a gift that won't send her sobbing from the room.*

*Kevin Cowherd*[1]

Richard has a problem: what should he get Lisa for her birthday. He is swamped at work; so he doesn't know when he will find time to get her a present. Besides he doesn't know what to get her. She has avoided all his questions about what she would like. "Oh, honey, I don't really care; anything will be fine," she says. But after ten years of marriage and a considerable number of gift occasions, he knows better than to believe this. He also knows the look of disappointment he saw when he gave her the last present. "Where's the card?" she asked. He said, "Oh, come on. You know who it's from. I just gave it to you."

He remembers the chill in the room, so he wants to make things a little more special and thoughtful this time.

Richard's problem is not unique. It demonstrates many of the gift dilemmas faced by men:

- First, finding out what will please the woman in your life is often not easy.

- Second, how does a busy man make it all happen?

- Third, you suspect that there is more to the story than just boxes, tissue paper and ribbon. But what?

Well, we as women are about to break the female code of silence and let you in on the secret story behind women and gifts. Then we will tell you ways to make the task easier, more romantic, and more satisfying to both of you. All of this will be covered in Part I called "For Him".

The second part of the book, called "For Her", will cover some of the same material, but it is addressed to a female audience. Be forewarned that if you read each other's portion, you will get some duplication.

The second half of the book talks to women about the part they play in the gift problem. We discovered how often women did not realize that what they said or did not say was adding to the confusion. For example, we heard, "Oh, it would spoil it if I had to ask him for something in particular." Or even this mind reading expectation, "If he really cares about me, he will just know what I want." And finally, "I never let him know if I don't like what he has given me. I just put it away."

So what do women want? We will try to tell you.

**Caution:**

Many of you will be inclined to go straight to the section called "Problem Solvers", chapters aimed at specific problems, (how to shop for specific items, last minute solutions, etc.). Be our guest. This is an important part of the book. It is very likely, though, that a woman in your life gave you this book. What did she have in mind? How is she trying to help you? What is she trying to tell you through this book? Of course, she would be pleased if you were more comfortable with the mechanics (notes and presentation, for example). But let us assure you, as women ourselves, that the problem is more complex than just the mechanics. The women in your lives would also like you to understand why men and women so often see the whole gift giving process differently. That is what we cover in the first four chapters of the book.

So once the crises is over, come back and read the early chapters. Here is where the behind-the-scenes stuff is revealed.

# For Him

# Why Is There a
# Problem?

# 1:  Unraveling the Mystery

*It isn't just about shopping for a gift; that's just the tip of the iceberg.*

*Anon. woman interviewee*

---

## Secret Scripts

The first piece of the mystery is that there is a *secret* script that women have about gifts. Often they haven't identified it, but it is there. Simply put, women long for something MAGIC to happen through your gift. They want to experience a special feeling of warmth, they want to feel that someone (you) truly knows them, AND that unusual care has been taken  to select a gift that reflects this insight. On top of all this, they would love a scene that only a Hollywood script writer could conceive — a package straight from a design studio — special lighting and music suitable to the occasion. In other words, they dream of a total and perfect experience.

As you can imagine, this rarely happens in real life to any of us, male or female.

## We Don't See It the Same Way

There are some other hidden aspects of gift giving we should alert you to. For example, have you noticed that men and women don't view gifts the same way?  We tried to find a man's observation on this difference.  We had to search hard to find anything written from a man's point of view on this topic.  This one from Robert Masello's, "What Guys Don't Get About Gift Giving, " *Mademoiselle*, July, 1984 said it best.

> Even today's most understanding men do
> not even begin to comprehend how much
> more presents mean to women than they do
> to men.  Or how certain holidays, like
> birthdays or Valentine's Day pack an
> emotional wallop that we don't feel ... the
> size of the gift is entirely peripheral.  I am
> saying that we men are often slow to realize
> the significance a woman will attach, and
> read into, a gift we give — as a result, we
> wind up giving gifts that send all kinds of
> signals we never intended to send.[2]

Someone has told this man inside information about the hidden meanings of gifts.  He appreciates the huge differences between the way men and women see gifts.

**Layered Meaning**

The rest of the story is even more complicated.  All gifts are layered with meanings to women.  They see gifts as mysteries to be solved.  She will examine and question your gift for clues to the relationship more thoroughly than an Agatha Christie detective.  What does it say about how he sees me?  How does he feel about me?  How is our relationship doing?  What's special in the gift that says our relationship is still important?   Do I still intrigue him ?"

These layers of meaning aren't something that happen only to adults.  You probably remember yourself as a child, worrying over the message implied by a Valentine that you sent.  Will she misunderstand?  Will she think you are silly?  What if the curly haired girl sends you a mushy card and your send her just a regular card?

So the gift giving process can be dangerous, and open to misunderstanding and disappointments even as early as the grade

14

school level. At this point in your life you would like to think you are beyond that. Probably not.

Misread messages still worried and plagued a number of men we talked with. Frank told of giving his wife an alluring negligee. He thought he was sending a message about her desirability. Unfortunately, she responded with tears. Much later he learned that she felt he thought her not sexy enough and was sure he was criticizing her at a time when she felt overwhelmed with motherhood and a new job.

We think Frank could have sent his true message more clearly if he had taken one more small step and written a note to go with the present. (See Chapter 14 on Notes.)

**The Romantic Dream**

There is still one more hidden aspect of gift giving. Many a woman sees herself as a romantic. Romantics believe we should all care as desperately as the loving couple in O. Henry's "The Gift of the Magi." Remember in that story, the husband and wife each sacrificed something of extreme value to provide a special gift for the other. This oft-told tale has become the unconscious standard some women use to calibrate the romance quotient in your gift. Tough standard, isn't it?

Writer Susan Jacoby clarified this overly romantic and unrealistic approach in her article on "Hidden Messages in Gifts."

> In a lover's gift we hope to find a trace of
> what we want from love itself - the
> recognition of a deeply felt wish that no
> one else has discerned - a wish we may
> even have failed to recognize in
> ourselves.[3]

Or as Dawn Bryan, author of *The Art and Etiquette of Gift Giving*, put it more simply, "The hunger for gifts is a hunger for approval, importance, affection and love."[4]

This is what you are up against!

Whether or not these attitudes are realistic, they often do exist, and to improve your gift giving, you need to be aware of them as you move toward a more loving gift giving strategy.

One male writer offered this insight into gift selection for a loved one that may start you thinking differently;

> As I see it, the appropriateness of a ... gift is
> a recognition and affirmation of the other
> person's qualities, his or her tastes, habits,
> needs, enthusiasms or pleasures. There is an
> intimacy implicit in things themselves that
> only two people who know each other very
> well can understand.[5]

Odd as it may sound, the gift of a pair of field glasses to the bird watcher or a gold thimble for the needlepointer may be more personal and thoughtful than a fine gold necklace.

The same writer tells a personal story that illustrates his point. After casually mentioning that he had never owned a decent shaving brush, he received a beautiful and expensive one on his next birthday. "Every time I used that brush, I felt lathered in understanding. My wife was a woman who regarded me as a *subject worthy of study and research*." Perhaps that captures the wish we heard from women as to how **they** want to be gifted.

By now you are probably wishing it weren't all so complicated. Professor Higgin's line from *My Fair Lady* comes to mind, "Oh, why can't a woman be more like a man?" What? And spoil the surprises?

# 2: The Misleading Guidelines

Women's hidden agendas are not the only thing that confuse the gift giving issue. Some of the gift problem stem from our use of some old and often contradictory guidelines. Take a second look at these familiar sayings:

A) Buy something that you would like; she will be sure to like it too.

B) Jewelry is alway easy and appropriate. (You can never go wrong with jewelry.)

C) ALL women love _____ ,perfume, lace, pink. You get the idea.

D) Mature adults don't need gifts to show their caring

E) Only something major and expensive is appropriate

Let's take these one by one.

A) You are two separate people. She has her own tastes and fondnesses. Do you like the same color, read the same books, order the same food in restaurants? Part of the specialness of gifting, as we see it, is attending to someone enough to discover her unique preferences and then giving her a gift with these in mind.

B) Jewelry was the subject of much discussion in our study groups. We learned that: 1) not all women like jewelry; 2) many worry that you will overspend; and 3) they have widely varying tastes; some like modern settings, some traditional, some more exotic. To avoid an expensive goof, we recommend that you read our section on buying her jewelry.

C) All women love ____ ( fill in the blank) is as outlandish as the ONE-SIZE-FITS-ALL designation on clothes. This fill in the blank statement is the ultimate in lack of attention to the woman's special qualities.

D) No one would deny the literal truth of the "we don't need gifts to show caring" statement. Of course, we don't NEED them. Of course, material evidence in the form of gifts is not essential to true feelings. But, honestly, aren't gifts visual symbols and reminders that most of us cherish?

Gifts are the little extras that enrich a relationship. These include "free gifts" such as compliments, as well as the wrapped present. Both types of gifts reduce the feelings of being taken for granted which are such a danger in any long standing relationship.

As a last comment we want to emphasize that it is not necessary to use "major credit card busters" to gift someone effectively. But we believe along with author/therapist Nathaniel Branden that it is romantic to express love materially too.

**It is the thought that counts.**

Mom was right when she taught us all that. We need to give full measure, though, to the *thinking* part. Think about the woman you are gifting. Who is she? What truly pleases her? How can I make this gift special? These are the essential questions. Be sure to address them fully.

We all, men and women, want to feel that someone has taken time to think about us.

# 3: What Men Told Us

In gathering information for this book, we asked men to respond to a questionnaire. Some of their comments were so insightful, and clarified so much, that we wanted you to see them. We wanted you to see the recurring themes. We also hoped that by reading a variety of stories you would be inspired to talk with your spouse or lover about her views. Maybe you would even use these questions as a springboard in your conversation. We firmly believe that there is a lot to be gained if each of you talk about how you feel about gifting.

**QUESTION: What would you like to know to make gift giving easier?**

We weren't surprised to learn that many men wanted to know about the same things.

- How to find out what she really wants.
- How to deal with someone who won't tell you what she wants.
- Ways to be unique when there is very little time.
- How to shop for " women things."
- Why are our expectations so far apart?

We promise to answer all these concerns.

**QUESTION: Where did your gift patterns start?**

# Gift Giving -- From Him to Her

There seemed to be two sources for men's patterns: 1) their families, particularly their mothers and 2) their wives.

"I really wasn't aware of the issue of gifts until I married. My wife, who is very generous, opened up a whole new view for me."

"When I got married, I expected to do presents at holidays just like we had done in my family. Surprise! So did my wife. More surprising was the fact that she expected gift things from me that I'd never seen my family do. My mom was delighted with any kind of gift wrapping. Nancy was shocked at the "casual ribbon" I tended to get by with when I was a kid."

"I learned from a mother who is very sensitive about the nature of gifts. She taught us that all gifts should be well thought out. This has had a good side in that I really get involved with the gift. As an adult, though, the problem comes when I don't have time to get this involved. Then I feel a little guilty. This adds a little stress to my holidays."

"In our family my father always had one big present for my mother and loved dropping hints for weeks ahead of time. He really loved the drama of it."

"I never saw my parents exchange gifts. I had lots to learn the first year I was married."

"It always seemed that my mother was in charge of all gift buying. Although she always signed Dad's name, I don't think he knew what was in the package any more than I did. I expected to fall into this same role. Janet had different patterns. She wanted me involved."

As men described their early experiences their views suddenly made sense. If they had trouble buying gifts, it was not a personal failing — they were merely repeating their early patterns. After these discussions, many men said that they wanted to tell their wives what they had discovered and to ask their wives for a picture of their family patterns.

Ask yourself some of these questions to bring back your early experiences with gifts:

1. Who bought the major gifts?

2. Who wrapped them?

3. What comments do you remember being made about gifts?

4. Was it better to give or to receive?

5. Any early disappointments? How did you deal with them?

6. What was a required response?

7. What occasions warranted a gift?

8. Was surprise important?

9. How did your family respond to your early efforts?

**QUESTION: How do you know if your gift is a success?**

"By the way her face lights up."

"It's not exchanged, it's used, it's displayed."

"If she's happy I know I'm in the ballpark; if she raves I'm on the mark; if she looks at me as she did on our first date, I've hit a home run."

After listening to many men tell about their struggles with gifts from how to find out what she wants, to how to find time to get it, we felt we understood your desire to please with your present. We also noted that you would like your efforts to be appreciated even when the gift isn't exactly perfect. You resented having your attempts discounted.

These points seemed important for women to know. So we are passing them along in the women's portion of this book. We also are telling her that you like to see her eyes light up, that you like to get a smile, a hug and a kiss. We know from talking with women that they aren't sure how to show you their appreciation and need a few tips.

## QUESTION: Which holidays and occasions call for a gift?

"I didn't know that Valentine's Day was for gifting. This created a huge problem. Sarah thought I didn't have any romantic feelings toward her because I ignored the day."

Here again family history seemed to influence your responses. The gift giving occasions covered a wide range:

> Traditional holidays
> Absolutely anything that is the anniversary of a first time
> Birthdays and anniversaries
> Valentine's Day
> Mother's Day
> When I am in trouble
> Spur of the moment

It is probably a good idea to check out each other's feelings on some of these sensitive dates. Find out more about the expectations that you each hold. The following stories are examples from couples who had different expectations.

Marybeth, whose husband is a busy executive in a start-up company, was embarrassed to tell us how disappointed she was that he didn't bring her a "pressy" on the birth of their first child. You can bet the second birth was noted!

Allison always marks Ted's calendar to remind him of the anniversary of their engagement, "because that was the start of everything." This is an important occasion for her.

Alan had a terrible time on their first Easter as a family. His reserved family background had not prepared him for Marta's family's style of celebration. Decorations, egg hunts, special spring presents were totally foreign to him. He felt more than a little uncomfortable since he wasn't sure what part he should play or what sort of gift fit this new scheme of things.

Another view that demonstrates the value of uncovering expectations came from a husband who loved gifting his wife except on one traditional occasion — Mother's Day. (This was a childless second marriage for both, although each had children from a previous marriage.) He explained, "She's not my mother, and besides it spoils the uniqueness of our relationship."

# 4: More of What Men Told Us

*The inappropriate gift is a little tragedy in human relations.*

*Anatole Broyard*[6]

---

There were two other questions that men answered on our questionnaire.

**QUESTION: What was the worst gift?**

The stories about the gifts that failed made us laugh and sigh for the missed connections.

An attractive, single woman we interviewed decided to stop seeing a successful business man she was dating because (among other reasons) he was prone to bringing her practical, irrelevant, last minute "drug store items " — a bar of soap, hand cream, a bag of hard candies. None of these items had any connection to her tastes or their relationship.

> Win a raffle, contest or lottery and you're
> exulted. But get an unexpected gift from
> someone and you're uneasy. "What's this
> for?" An ungracious response perhaps, but
> perfectly human and natural.[7]

It is just these little tragedies that we hope to avoid with this book. The men in our discussion groups had some interesting stories that we want to pass along.

The worst gift? The one I totally forgot to get one anniversary. Now I mark my calendar a week before just to make sure I have time.

Early in our marriage I actually believed her when she said, "I don't want anything for my birthday." Bad judgement on my part.

I thought I was so clever one year. Her birthday and our anniversary are only a few days apart, so I planned one big combination gift that I gave her on her birthday which came first. That year's anniversary had a sort of sad hollow ring to it.

Then there were specific gifts that seemed to lack the charm the giver expected.

Marvin thought he had a real winner. He and his family had recently gone in for camping in a big way. They had purchased a tent trailer, cook stove, sleeping bags, etc.. He decided a dandy gift for Maria would be a portable toilet. She didn't agree.

---

Gadgets can be tricky business. One husband we talked with was puzzled at the lack of enthusiasm for a motorized foot massager he gave his wife. He knew she loved having her feet rubbed, so why the disappointment? He learned later that, yes, she did enjoy having her feet rubbed, but the personal caring and conversation that came with it was even more important. This gadget made him seem impersonal and distant.

---

The story that we really liked was this one. Dean knew these facts: his wife wanted a waffle iron, he loved surprises, and they needed a new garbage can. So to disguise the waffle iron, he buried it in the new garbage can and wrapped the whole package. "You can tell you goofed when your wife is still telling the story a decade later," he told the group.

"What woman doesn't like rubies?" thought Jim as he purchased the largest gift he had ever bought, a diamond and ruby engagement ring. Answer: his bride-to-be didn't like rubies. Fortunately, they were able to clear this up very early and she is still wearing the diamond engagement ring — no rubies, thank you — they selected together. And they learned very early in their relationship how to handle misses.

In the woman's half of this book we talk to women about this sensitive issue of disappointing gifts. We urge the two of you to share your thoughts, doubts and preferences on this topic.

**QUESTION: What Was the Best Gift?**

Three stories were particularly interesting examples of creative gifting.

Devin described himself as someone who loved to create surprises and suspense around presents. Because his wife usually managed to figure out ahead of time his gifts to her, he decided to make it a real challenge. He bet her $500 dollars she would not be able to guess this year's present. For the next couple of weeks she made dozens of guesses - all wrong - much to his delight. On Christmas morning, as she staggered sleepily into the living room, her husband and children were laughing and pointing at the ceiling. "Look up, Mom!" There, suspended from the ceiling, were 500 one dollar bills.

---

Peter spent several months in Europe shortly before his engagement to Rebecca. While he was there he kept a daily log of his adventures and his thoughts about her and their future together. His engagement present to her upon returning was to give her this personal journal where he had recorded his daily thoughts of caring for her.

---

When Darren proposed to his wife, he had plans for a special engagement ring, but he wanted it to be a surprise. So Donna

27

consented to be blindfolded at the jewelers while measurements were made for the wax impression. But Darren was not finished with his surprise. After the ring was completed, he invited her to a special dinner to talk about their plans. As an elegant gesture, he asked the waiter for two champagne cocktails. His bride-to-be was enjoying herself and talking so animatedly, she nearly missed the fact that he had arranged to have the ring hidden in the bottom of the champagne glass among the bubbles.

We are delighted to report these successes. It was such fun to hear men recount the happy feelings they and their wives felt.

One man did issue a **warning.** "You run into a hazard when you come up with a super gift. What do I do next time?"

Please don't worry about that. Most of the wives we talked to were quite happy recalling special gifts that had been given in previous years. No one seemed to expect a repeat performance on every occasion. So one particularly good gift could let you rest on your laurels for quite a while.

# 5: Fear of Shopping

*Gift giving requires gift purchasing, and gift
purchasing requires shopping, and one of the main
reasons men get married in the first place is so they
won't have to shop anymore.*

Esquire[8]

Now comes the sticky part. To give a gift you often have to go
SHOPPING. Unfortunately, we are not talking about
comfortable, familiar hardware stores or intriguing electronics
departments where you can browse with ease. We are talking
about territory Capt. James Kirk of *Star Trek* fame explores —
"Where no man has gone before."

In interviews, wives often mentioned that their husbands hated to
shop. It is easy to see why they dislike shopping. First there is the
unfamiliar territory problem, complete with foreign language.
What kind of word is "lingerie"? There are other equally foreign
phrases. Is she a "misses or junior" size? (Sounds like a value
judgment one should not make in a foreign land). "Is your wife a
summer or fall color palette?" (She always seemed like a year-
round person to you). Then there are all those strange numbers;
size 11-12, medium, 12, one-size-fits-all. Why can't it be more
precise you ask? Like 32 waist or 40 jacket. Or 2 by 4 lumber or
3/4" bolts? You've got us there. Better ask manufacturers.

To worsen this general discomfort, add a time crunch. When can
you do this task called shopping? Lunch hours are already too
short. After work? How do you explain being late if you are
trying for a surprise? Or in some cases, how do you get to the
specialty shop that closes at 5:00?

Holiday times only make it more difficult. Now you have to join the throngs of people trying to get their own right gifts. Some items such as red roses at Valentine's Day are completely sold out or have followed the economics of supply and demand and are outrageously priced. The aisles in most department stores are so crowded you can't move efficiently from counter to counter. Clerks, if you can find them, are deep in conversation with the shoppers who got there before you. Finally, check-out lines are indomitable.

Relax. We have some suggestions that can make this task less intimidating and perhaps even satisfying. We all like to do something effectively, particularly if it makes someone else take notice. If you want to produce presents with less strain, read on.

# Problem Solvers

# 6: How to Find Out What She Really Wants

*Man must never be judged according to the category to which he belongs. The category is the most barbarous and diabolical aberration ever begotten by human mind.*

G.V.Georghiu

---

If you already get it right 80 to 90% of the time, you can skip this chapter.

If your statistics are not that high, we would like to help you raise your chances for success.

One man we talked with said he really never asked his wife what she wanted. He just kept track of things that she admired throughout the year. Actually, we highly recommend this approach, but it does have some pitfalls. More than a few women we know exclaim over many things on a shopping excursion or a visit to a friend's house. They don't necessarily want these things for themselves; they are just expressing interest or delight in an object. They have told us that this is just fantasy time for them — mentally trying on a life style, an article of clothing, etc. Merely fun. They were surprised to learn that their husbands took all these statements as "wants." "No wonder he clams up when we go window shopping. He must feel overwhelmed by what he thinks are my expectations. He is always grumpy after one of our mall trips," said Susan in one of our discussion groups.

Listening for clues is a good way to learn what she wants unless she is like the woman described above. Then you need to check out her real interests; probably by asking some questions such as, "Is that something you would really like to have?"

Now suppose you haven't been tracking her wishes and hints throughout the year. How do you find out what she wants?

What's wrong with, "What do you want for your birthday, our anniversary, etc.?" Many of you told us that your wives reply, "Oh, anything you get will be just fine with me." That leaves you nowhere; so you must persevere.

First you need to know which approach you are dealing with. Here's where some catagories might help.

---

**Is she one of these?**

A) Those who don't _know_ what they want.
B) Those who won't _say_ what they want.
C) Those who _REALLY know_ what they want.

---

How to deal with each category.

### Category A

If she falls in **Category A (those who don't know),** you need to prime the pump. This can be done in a number of ways.

Give her either-or choices. Would you prefer a special dinner at our favorite restaurant or a brunch at the nicest hotel in town?

Get her to play "fantasy gift". What would she buy for herself if she won $50, $100, etc.?

Pull out catalogues and ask her to tear out suggestions to give you at regular intervals.

Try to get her to set categories such as clothes, personal treats, trips, hobby or collection items.

> **Encourage Her to Collect**
>
> "Show us a man whose wife gathers folk art, paperweights, cookie jars, pitchers, boxes, bottles, first editions, or busts of Napoleon, and we'll show you a guy who is never at loss for a gift."[9]

## Category B

If she falls in **Category B (those who won't say)**, ask her to read Chapter 24 on Myths in the other half of this book. In fact, read it with her. Until then, you can also:

Employ a spy to report on her secret desires. Children are often delighted to take on this job. Her friends might also like a cloak-and-dagger role.

Ask her to make notes or lists that she posts somewhere. She does not have to talk about what she wants and spoil the magic.

## Category C

If she falls in **Category C (those who really know)**, you might think buying her a gift would be a snap. But you are not home free. This group is usually very specific about their wants. They often have a particular brand name and item in mind.

Jeanne showed her husband an ad that featured a very special and expensive handbag that she wanted for her birthday. Unfortunately, Rick couldn't get to the store in the ad, so he went to another very chic store. Since it did not carry the brand she had mentioned, he selected another fine bag of equal quality that he figured would fill the bill.

When Jeanne opened the package, (the one she was so sure held the wished-for purse) she was troubled. The purse inside was one she had rejected earlier as not meeting her needs. What could she say without appearing overly fussy, ungrateful, or even spoiled?

The core of the problem with Category C is that you might not be able to track down the exact gift.  Here's when you ask for specifics — store, brand, picture.  Then save your self some effort by calling the store and asking them to hold the special item.

A small percentage of men said they absolutely refused to purchase a specific, predetermined item because it smacked too much of being given a shopping list.  If they are successful with their choices, we congratulate them.  We do suggest that they ask the receiver how she feels about this approach and listen carefully to the answer.

In general, men told us they appreciated being asked for something concrete; it assured them of success.  They did like a little flexibility — maybe two or three possibilities.  Having choices enabled them to express their taste as well as to preserve some element of surprise.

So how DO you include surprise for Category C?  Suppose she has asked for say, a "white summer coat."  Where do you find that?  What style? length? fabric?  This is becoming a mystery to you.

Try this.  When asked for a specific  item of clothing that you are uncertain about, plan an excursion to let her make her own selection.  You put on your best "shopping face" and accompany her.  Then if you want the surprise touch, you take her to lunch and have a flower delivered by the maitre'd or ask the kitchen to put a candle on a cupcake or a special dessert.  We know a couple who chose a bracelet together for a gift, and he insisted on carrying it out of the store.  At lunch he had arranged with the restaurant to present her with a white rose.  At that moment he officially gave her the package.

Or on this shopping trip, have her select three or four things that she likes.  You then arrange to have them held and go back later alone to pick up one of them.  She doesn't know for sure which to expect, but she can anticipate being pleased with any of them.  After all, she was involved with their choice.

Another problem can come up with a Category C. What if you balk at her suggestion? You know she already has 27 English tea cups and you think it totally pointless to get her another. Please remember you are trying to please HER wishes. Do they really have to make sense? This is not the time to lecture or editorialize.

# 7: What Type Is She?

Wouldn't it be nice if you could plug in some numbers to a computer and know about your wife's preferences? Well, the brain is a pretty good computer and you CAN take note of some facts by observing her manner. She probably will fit into one of the following four categories. (Thanks to Susan Scanlon of *Type Reporter*.)[10] [11]

A. " NO SURPRISES PLEASE"

B. PRACTICAL AND TRADITIONAL

C. SPUR OF THE MOMENT

D. GIFTS ARE SO SPECIAL

## No Surprises Please

Let us describe A's preferences first. The key is that she would much prefer to be in on the planning and selection of presents, even her own. Usually because she has a very specific present in mind. In addition, she relishes the anticipation, which represents part of the gift to her. She has an interest in gifts that will increase her knowledge or awareness. So what might you select for her?

If she has a favorite author, she would enjoy getting his or her latest work or one long out of print. You might try to find an autographed copy of an older book or have a contemporary author inscribe a new book to her. These women are also perfect candidates for a book store gift certificate.

With the "no surprises please" style you will not be out of line to have her participate in the selection of her own gift.

One of the authors, definitely an A, still tells about her October/December Christmas. One fall she wanted some specific clothes for her winter wardrobe and knew if she waited until Christmas to buy them or get them as presents two things would happen. First the selection would be greatly reduced and second, there would be a much shorter time in which to wear and enjoy them. Seasons change fast in California. So she said to her husband, "I know what I would like for Christmas — a fall shopping trip!" "Isn't it a bit early?" he responded.

She carefully explained how women are forced to buy clothes for one season before the season. So if she wanted to have a wide choice of winter clothing, wives had to select them in the fall.

The upshot was that they went Christmas shopping a week later in October. Then he asked if he should put these away for the next two and a half months. "Oh, no, I really love this new stuff and I want to get all the use out of it I can before the season is over."

"But what about Christmas morning?"

"Don't worry. I know exactly what to do about that." And she did. On Christmas Eve she wrapped the clothes beautifully and put them under the tree. He looked at her with bewilderment (he loves surprises) as she opened her packages the next morning. It took awhile, but she finally convinced him how special this gift was and that for her it was great fun to get the present twice, once in October and again in December. The author admits she is a bit extreme, but she was happy.

## Practical and Traditional

The second more easily recognized type is the woman who treasures getting something just a little better that what she would pick out for herself, yet not TOO extravagant. Something top quality that suits her — say a fine leather briefcase for her professional side or a really beautiful watch for a multitude of sides. She also values tradition and history; so long-standing family customs add to her enjoyment of any gift. Since she is usually the one who puts on the big productions for holidays and birthdays, she might appreciate a bit of a production being made for her.

Perhaps you could start a tradition just for her. For example, you could always give her a gift at certain special times — say the stroke of midnight or at the exact time you were married. Or the tradition could involve a certain place, such as sitting on the stairs. Presents that would be a reflection of her style might be to arrange a yearly family portrait, or to get some old family photos framed, or add something to her favorite collection. She likes memories too. One man we knew of gave his wife an anniversary luncheon that included all her former bridesmaids. You get the idea.

**Spur of the Moment**

The third style really doesn't get as excited over complicated events. Low key, spur-of-the moment is more to her liking. Usually she likes outdoor or physical gifts. She unlike some of the others might be a good candidate for a day at a spa or a massage. Any leisure time gifts could be appropriate for her — balloon rides, sports item, a new leotard, or a beach picnic. The element of surprise is definitely an important part of the gift for her. Another effective way to please her is to find something that appeals to her senses. How about a down comforter, a CD player, or piano lessons? Probably she enjoys getting many small gifts. This could be handled by breaking up a perfume set into soap, oils, perfume, and powder then wrapping them all separately.

**Gifts Are Special**

This last style may be the one who started the whole idea of hidden scripts.

She has in her mind a complete picture, or script, of how the whole gift process should go. After all, she puts hours of thought and planning into her gifts to other people and expects the same in return. She tries very hard to make the whole thing extra special. But this script of hers is seldom revealed to anyone. So your job is harder.

For her, gifts are important symbols of how someone sees her and how much thought they gave to understanding her. The potential for disappointment is high for her since she wants the gift to represent so much — caring and connection. She will particularly appreciate a personal note that says why the gift reminds you of her. Perhaps you chose the gift because it suggested a quality of hers you like. Tell her this. One husband married to this type gave his wife a large lace covered bed pillow with a note saying how it reminded him of her softness and femininity. This type also treasures the extra effort in the presentation. Fortunately, women in this style give a great response to gifts, making any effort or agonizing worth it.

We recently heard of a business that seemed to be in tune with the times and this style. The owners, two women, recognized that when people are busy it is very difficult to put together an elegant and romantic presentation or occasion. Their business involves handling all the details of a fanciful presentation for a set fee. The recipient gets to keep all the lovely props and accessories they use to create a scene — damask napkins, silver champagne bucket, lace tablecloth, etc.

Actually, in one form or another, this sort of service would be helpful for husbands of all these types we have described.

Of course, everyone is unique. We just thought it might be helpful to get a general picture of what four common styles of gift receivers you might find out there.

In some cases there may be some overlap, women who display two styles. We suggest that you talk this part over with your spouse or lover. Ask her which sounds the most like her. The point is not to surprise the "No Surprises" lady or forget to be extra attentive to the presentation for the "Gifts are Special" woman. "The Practical and Traditional" is likely to be uncomfortable with an elaborate set up that probably offends her practical side.

Talk it over, ask her, then select your approach.

# 8: Buying Her Clothing

"Buying clothes for her is risky business unless you know what you are doing," said one busy business executive who had tried buying her clothes without success on several occasions. "My advice is — forget it."

The women we interviewed had more complaints about gifts of clothing than any other category. Some of the stories were funny, but many indicated that shopping for clothes is a complicated activity. Although some women reported that they got tired even thinking about shopping, more told of their "born to shop" enthusiasm that we never heard from the men we talked to. Many women said they spent hours shopping for the perfect blouse to match a favorite suit. Clothes shopping to a woman can involve a whole set of criteria baffling to a man whose idea of shopping is find it, pay for it, leave. Ten minutes.

You've now been forewarned that buying something for her to wear will be difficult. Below is information to help you if you really want to try this.

## Clothing Facts

**Size:** Men's sizes are a snap to you, clear-cut and standard, i.e., a 16 1/2  33 shirt. Period. But women's!  As a guide:

**A Regular or Misses dress size** is for the well-proportioned figure with even sizes. (2 - 16) Merle Streep probably wears a Regular size.

**Junior sizes** designed for the youthful figure of any age are odd numbered sizes. ( 3 - 13) Barbara Mandrel is a Junior.

**Woman's sizes** are for the full-figured body and usually run in half sizes. (14 1/2 or l6 1/2) Rosemary Clooney would fit into this category.

**Petite sizes** are shorter in the waist, the sleeves, the legs, and the rise. Both mother Debbie Reynolds and daughter Carrie Fisher are petites.

To make it even more complex, standards are lax and each designer/manufacturer cuts differently. So your spouse may say a size 10 fits perfectly if it's a Liz Clairborne. But if it's a Ralph Lauren, she'll probably wear an 8. You're not likely to know all that unless you ask her.

**Designers:** If your spouse likes clothes, she'll know about designers and what each line produces each season. So will her friends. These friends just might be your ally when it comes to making clothes suggestons. Check with the ones whose taste she has told you she admires.

**Color:** In recent years personal coloring has played big all over the country as women have become aware of what colors flatter them the most. Your spouse may have "had her colors done" and carry around a packet of colors she matches when she shops. Many men don't understand that there's a complicated art in choosing flattering colors and color combinations. Before you shop for her, ask her to put together a small packet of colors she especially likes for you to take with you.

**Style:** Forever changing. Most of the men told us that fashion is a total puzzlement to them dreamed up by an industry out to make money. Probably true, but women do like to have gifts of something that is new in the fashion world. Any good sales person will help you with this. But once again, look before you leap. Take a good look at the type of clothes your significant other wears. If she always wears suits to work, a gauze number might not be for her, even if the sales clerk vows every women on earth wants one.

So, if the woman in your life cannot find that blouse she wants in several hours of visiting a dozen stores and trying on everything that looks feasible, how can you expect to succeed in ten minutes? "All he knows," said Susan at one of our interviews, "is that I'd like a new blouse." Any blouse will not do and will probably cause disappointment all around. (If we switched the scene to a hardware store, any hammer would not do it either.)

It's our observation that clothing has sometimes been a catch-all gift for many years in some relationships. Merchants understand this and therefore make it very easy to exchange. Sam put it this way, "It doesn't matter much what I buy as long as it's in the ball park, since we both know she'll exchange it anyway."

Of course, some men are experts in choosing items that delight. They seem to have both knack and knowledge confounding to other men in the group we interviewed. Are we suggesting you either have that knack or you don't? Maybe so. Men who have this ability shop carefully. One told us that if he knew his wife wanted a blouse to coordinate with a skirt or jacket he always took that piece with him to be sure of the right match. Do you do that?

What clothing would please her? Women mentioned specific clothing items that had pleased them immensely. The winners were:

> **Leather Goods** especially handbags, belts. Remember to have her show you what shape and design she likes.

**Any Complete Outfit** Anything from a jogging suit to a three-piece designers ensemble, all matched.

**Beautiful Scarves** Large ones in lush colors are especially popular with most women.

**A Special Coat** Yes, mink did come up — but so did interesting rain or woolen coats, coats for the ski country and silk evening coats.

**Lingerie** Men like to give this gift and women like to receive it. It is important to know her size and what colors she likes best.

**Sweaters** There's a wide selection from light-weight cotton to luxurious, expensive cashmere. There is something to fit all budgets. Choose a roomy version.

**Furs** At one time, as a dream luxury item, a mink coat went right along with a Rolls Royce and a Big Diamond. But times change, and fur items have become controversial as environmental concerns have grown. Endangered animals are not in the same category as domestically raised mink, but the wearer can be hassled on the street for either. For cold weather, nothing quite matches the warmth of fur, but if your wife has strong opinions about this, you could make a major mistake. So be sure a fur coat would please her before you take the plunge.

**Personal Shopping Guide**

Finally, when you do go shopping for clothes for her, be prepared. Give your love a 3 x 5 card like the one pictured below and ask her to complete it. She'll think you're brilliant and thoughtful and you'll have all the needed information available to go do battle in the boutique.

---

**SANDRA'S CLOTHING LIST**

**Measurements:** Waist, Bust, Hips
**Dress Size:** Size 8, Petite (short waisted)
**Skirt Size:** Size 8, Petite
**Blouse:** Size 6, Petite
**Sweater:** Petite Medium
**Lingerie:** Size 8 or S if SML
**Colors:** Blue, Black, Soft Pink
**Likes:** A Classic Look
**Comments:** Avoid anything too fussy, no ruffles
**Favorite stores:** Suzanne's Boutique. Ask for Margie

---

**Guaranteed Success**

The most successful over-all strategy for successful clothing gift buying was expressed in a number of different versions. Peter set aside an afternoon to be with his wife. He told her to pick out her favorite store, choose items she liked and have them set aside. After taking her to lunch, he then picked out his favorite from those she tried on for him. He had them wrapped and later give them to her for their anniversary. Bruce did the same thing. Only he asked her to wear the new clothes right out of the store to dinner. Many stores today are geared to helping with such a shopping project. The big ones all have a Personal Shopping Department. You can call, set up an appointment time and tell the shopper what, in general, you'd like to see in your price range. On the day of the event you sit back in comfort, over your coffee, while your spouse models for you. We've never met a woman who wouldn't like an experience like this!

In summary then, gifts of clothing are among the most complicated to achieve, yet often the most rewarding. Remember what she probably wants is the interest you show in what's she wearing.

# 9: Buying Her Jewelry

*Dumb jewels often in their silent kind, More than quick words, Do move a woman's mind.*

Shakespeare

---

As an important gift item, you can't go wrong with jewelry. **Unless it's the wrong jewelry.**

The Wall Street Journal said it in a cover story entitled "Dust Busters Aren't Forever, Jewels Are."[12] They emphasized that, by and large, men don't comprehend the importance, the anticipation, the symbolism women place on gifts. And nowhere is this more evident than with jewelry.

Jewelry is considered a significant present — for the important times. For many women jewelry carries the message, "He loves me. This shows it because jewelry is **permanent**." Men don't always understand all this, but they do sense the importance women place on it.

Jewelry for women fails into three categories

1. Real jewelry, the diamonds, gold, emeralds, sapphires and rubies that have been so desirable throughout history.

2. Semi-precious gems are usually more reasonably priced, but not less attractive.

3. Trendy and costume jewelry is fun for women to wear and available in all price ranges.

Ordinarily real and semi-precious jewelry is reserved as gifts for the big occasions like a 25th anniversary, while the trendy and costume works for the fun times like a birthday or a promotion.

The question is simple. How do you choose the jewelry that will make her eyes light up? Women have asked us to tell you the following.

## 1. Real Jewelry

For a women a gift of real jewelry is often very symbolic of the relationship — a fact that men recognize, but don't always understand. This is especially true of rings. Engagement, wedding, and anniversary symbolize the never-ending circle of love. Remember that "Diamonds are a girl's best friend" as Marilyn Monroe used to sing.

So you need to select real jewelry with care. Any good jeweler will give you detailed information.about what you want to buy. Diamonds, for example, are graded by size, color, cut and perfection and the prices reflect all that. Ditto emeralds, rubies and sapphires. Ask about the differences.

Real jewelry is an investment. Today a top quality one carat diamond, for example, is worth several thousand dollars but, as the ads say, "Diamonds are forever." The same diamond could have been purchased in 1920 for a tenth the price. Jewelry pieces are often handed down generation to generation.because of their financial and sentimental value.

Real jewelry requires understanding the needs of your spouse. If you miss on the flowers or the lingerie, it's not a big deal, but a miss on a major hunk of gems and gold can be serious. We heard some interesting stories.

Amy wanted diamonds for their 25th wedding anniversary and suggested several times that diamond studded earrings would be nice. Her husband heard the diamond part. On their anniversary he proudly presented her with a large necklace with her name spelled in diamonds — a very expensive piece of jewelry intended to show his affection. Amy is a quiet person whose taste is classic and subdued. This gift was a real shock to her.

The suggestions below have been recommended in other parts of this book, but they are of particular importance in buying a major piece of jewelry.

- Take time to shop carefully.

- Talk to her best friends about what she really wants.

- Carefully note which pieces of jewelry she wears the most as a good guideline for what would please her.

- Choose something that symbolizes your relationship.

- Do have the piece engraved. The engraving may be as important to her as the gift itself.

## 2. Semi-precious jewelry

These jewels are often as desirable as the more costly real. Many women told us they'd prefer a large jade piece than a small cluster of diamonds or rubies. Some would prefer a five-carat aquamarine pin rather than a half-carat ruby. The price would be about the same. Since most men are not as likely to be acquainted with the semi-precious stones and minerals, they may not be as likely to consider these as good choices.

Literally thousands of minerals are used as semi-precious gems. As a guide, below are some of the best know of these gems in the most popular colors. Take a look at some of them the next time you go to a jewelry store.

**Aquamarine** — Blue-green and transparent, often several carats
**Amethyst** — Deep purple or violet color quartz
**Topaz** — A smoky yellow gem
**Garnet** — Deep red transparent (there's an ancient belief that the wearer would be unaffected by wine)
**Tourmaline** — A lavender-pink stone
**Quartz** — Best known in its colorless form, comes in

53

colored varieties as well

**Turquoise** — Typically a bluish-green stone popular in the Southwest

**Moonstone** — Milk-white translucent gem with a pearl luster

**Opal** — A stone capable of reflecting light in a play of colors

**Jade** — A hard stone, usually shades of green or white

**The Organic Gems**

**Amber** — A Brownish-yellow translucent fossil, lightweight

**Coral** — From the tropical reefs, yellowish pink

**Jet** — A deep lustrous, hard, black stone

**Pearl** — From the oyster, one of the world's favorites.

Pearls are so popular they need a category unto themselves. You probably know that cultured pearls are made by inserting a piece of sand in an oyster. The oyster is later harvested for the pearl. Pearls are graded according to size, shape and color with the larger and the most perfect being the most valuable. Matching the beads figures into the cost of a pearl necklace as well. Uneven pearls, called *baroque*, are less expensive, but not necessarily less desirable as many women, especially older women, find them more flattering.

Pearls must be selected with care since there is a thriving racket in fake pearls. These are glass beads that have been dipped in a pearl coating that chips off after wearing. Pearls come in many shades of cream from very white to peach to blue. Black pearls are not really black, but grey. It's good to choose a color most flattering to your loved one's skin tone. Since pearls are so expensive, good copies are available in nearly all department stores in all sizes and lengths. Barbara Bush wears her simulated pearls with pride.

**3. Costume jewelry**

Jewelry is trendy and follows fashion. This can be a big

problem for a man who doesn't pay much heed to fashion and who is buying for a spouse who does. As this book is written, jewelry tends to make a statement: big and bold. Some years ago small circle pins of precious stones were the rage. Today's trendy, big jewelry will probably be fake — a pearl choker of big beads, large costume earrings and big colorful pins. These interesting fake pieces might be your choice for fun presents on less important occasions.

**Pricing: Retail/Wholesale.**

Women told us there's another problem regarding jewelry, that is, the price. There is a huge mark-up in retail jewelry. Many shoppers prefer to avoid the mark-up by shopping at a wholesale distributor. This can create a problem for a busy man who knows he is not an expert and feels more comfortable buying from a reputable jeweler. Women often told us that they were more likely than their mates to know about buying wholesale and felt disappointed with a small gem when they knew they could get twice as much for the money at the wholesale market.

Mark told us he had the solution to the wholesale jewelry dilemma. "Somewhere you have a friend who can buy for you on the wholesale market — and while you're at it, ask him to find you a beautiful box to put it in." And what woman can resist a pale blue box from Tiffany's?

**Birthday stones**

Custom has it that we have a gem for every month of the year. Buying a piece of jewelry with a birthday gem often makes a good gift. In addition to birthstone rings, there are birthstone pendants, earrings, pins.

> **January** — garnet
> **February** — amethyst
> **March** — bloodstone
> **April** — diamond
> **May** — emerald
> **June** — pearl

**July** — ruby or onyx
**August** — carnelian
**September** — sapphire or chrysolite
**October** — beryl, aquamarine or opal
**November** — topaz
**December** — ruby

### Jewelry from other sources

For some beautiful items that are often less expensive, consider bracelets from woods, pins from bone and items from ceramics, steel and glass, even papier mache. All can be made into jewelry works of art. There is much more of a variety than there used to be.

### Gold and Silver

If it's gold she likes, remember it comes in carats depending on the amount of other metals mixed with the gold. Twenty-four carat is the purest gold, and has a rich warm color. It is often too soft for jewelry. Fourteen carat is somewhat less expensive and has a cooler color — eighteen is in-between. Gold-filled is metal with a gold coating, much less expensive and less desirable since the coating can wear off. Also watch for the weight of the gold. Solid pieces are more expensive than those that are hollow. Some hollow gold bracelets, for example, are beautiful until nicked and then are very hard to repair. Silver is less expensive than gold, but not less attractive. Silversmiths create beautiful work today. You're in luck if your spouse has white hair since silver looks especially good on such women. Younger women often look better in jewelry that has a polished shine; older women may look best in metals with a texture often called "brushed" or "Florentine."

### Settings

Settings are a very important part of jewelry. Here is where finding a good jewelry maker can be of great value to you. Jewelry making has always been an art form. Today you can find some remarkable work done by street artists. Look at fairs if you have the time to browse and poke. Most jewelry stores, of course, have designers in house. Finding a designer whose work you and your partner both like can make your selection 100% easier. Designer settings also give you a chance to have something personal, like initials or an important date engraved. Since some jewelry constitutes such a major present, you may want to choose unset gems and return with your spouse at a later date to design or pick out a setting. That way you are sure she'll have what will please her. And we've never yet met a woman who wouldn't like a trip to the jewelry store with her partner.

# 10: Buying Her Perfume

*Promise her anything, but give her Arpege*

---

One look at the slick, extravagant sales promotion layouts and you know that "little" gift of perfume that may only be a little oil essence from a rose or herb, a drop of musk, and plenty of plain old alcohol will cost you money. Because it is a lucrative business, "stars" frequently lend their names to the market, such as Misha, Cher, Julio. In addition, the major designers nearly all have their own perfumes like Calvin Klein's "Eternity" or Hermes' "On the Rock's". Virtually every cosmetic company has a whole line of perfumes, each with another provocative name, Estee Lauder's "White Linen", for example. All this makes the perfume counters appear flooded and only adds more confusion to the man trying to buy his partner a small bottle of fragrance.

Since perfume selection is difficult, our advice, if you don't know what you're doing, is to pause a minute before you pull out the credit card. Read on.

Perfume is a lovely gift — one of the most intimate and desirable when it's the right choice. Perhaps it's just because so many men miss on this one, that she's likely to really be delighted when your choice pleases her. The beautiful packaging, the unusual bottles, are part of the offering. Women are rightfully charmed by these beautiful bottles — a gift in themselves.

## What to do? Essential Information on Perfume:

**Cheap perfumes can make you sick.** Literally. Inexpensive perfumes with a strong, reeking scent will definitely not make the sort of impression you are hoping for. You don't want to give an offensive gift!

**Because of the chemistry of the skin, the same perfume will not smell the same on each person.** Wise women, when shopping for a new perfume, will try a sample on their wrists or temples and leave it on all morning to see how it reacts and how long it will last. What if you like it — and she doesn't? What if she likes it — and you don't? Time for some home-spun, down-to-earth, communication. You like a perfume, but you don't know what the scent might be like on her? Steer her by the perfume counter the next time you're out shopping/browsing together. Put a drop of your choice on her wrist. Don't be surprised if you don't find a new one she likes right away — there may be many on the market, but it will probably take a while to find one that works for her.

**Unlike younger women, women of a certain age, are more often quite loyal to their long time preferences.** These women usually wear only two or three brands consistently. They, therefore, are easy to buy for. You can either ask her the names of her favorite perfumes or take a peek at the names on the bottles she uses most often.

**Perfumes can be seasonal.** Some women prefer a lighter, flower scent reserved for warm weather and a heavier muskier scent for the winter time. Sometimes they chose a "career" favorite for day time and another for going out on the town.

**Many women don't like to mix their scents.** Some like their powder and soap and toilet water to be the same scent as their perfume. "Too confusing otherwise," they tell us. So be sure that fancy boxed perfumed soap matches her perfume.

**Most of the well-known perfumes have been around a long time.** Particularly the French ones like Chanel No. 5, Arpege, Joy,

J'Vien, L'Air du temps, Lanvin, etc. are time-tested classics. All the newer perfumes seem to be a take off on the old ones. You're safer with the tried and true. And some women will **only** wear French perfumes. They are convinced those perfumes are superior. The French intend to keep it that way.

**Know the difference between perfume and cologne and toilet water (eau du toilette).** Cologne and toilet water are perfumes to which alcohol has been added so, to the uninformed, it looks like you're getting much more for the money. The bottles don't always tell you either. Colognes and toilet water are refreshing for a splash after a bath, but they fade fast.

**Avoid giving her the same scent an old flame used to wear.**

**If you don't know the name of what she wears, ask her.** Contrary to what many men seem to think, women love to have men comment on their perfume. They are pleased to be asked about their choice.

**Perfumes don't last forever — a year, maybe two.** Perfumes, like flowers, are better fresh. Have you ever been crunched in a seat at the opera next to a woman whose perfume has gone stale? Unless your lady-love bathes in it, small bottles work out better. A well-known merchant told us about a client who one anniversary delighted his wife with 5 large bottles of the finest French perfumes. The next year he came again to repeat the order that had so pleased her. Needless to say, she had barely make a dent in the first order.

**Buy quality and buy it in the small sizes.** And **do** go to the trouble. Women love to get the perfume they love to wear.

# 11: Flowers for M'Lady

Men sense that the women in their lives love to get flowers. Or do they?

All flowers are not alike. In fact, some have no appeal as gifts at all. Women tell us that men don't always understand the differences in flower choices and could use some enlightenment.

## The most popular flowers

**Roses** When thinking of flowers to send to their lady loves, most men reach for a dozen long stems. Florists tells us that red roses are the favorite by far. We were surprised then to learn during our interviews with women, that one long-stemmed perfect red rose (with or without a crystal vase) often symbolized love more than a whole dozen, especially on Valentine's Day. Potted miniature roses make a longer lasting gift.

**Carnations** Favorites for some, not so popular for others. These are long lasting and colorful but not considered very romantic.

**Daisies** For a fresh garden look, these are forever popular and nearly always available at a reasonable price. Do buy several bunches. One little wimpy bunch of 99 cent daisies is not going to do a thing.

**Orchids** In purple or white they make superb corsages and small potted ones last for weeks.

**Tulips** These colorful flowers are the very essence of spring. Consider buying these in pots also.

**Gardenias** The gardenia is often used in corsages because of its wonderful aroma. Be aware that the gardenia bruises very easily.

Most of you know the value of finding a good broker you can trust. The same goes for a good florist. You want one that can be reached by phone and paid by credit card. You'd be surprised at the confidence that can result from spending some time at a florist's shop meeting the florist and becoming acquainted with the wide selection available. This should not be a farm-and-garden store that peddles fertilizer, shrubs, peat moss, along with a handful of flowers, but rather a place where cut flowers and potted plants dominate. When you find such a shop, it pays to eyeball everything, ask the names, take some notes. Find out if the flowers you think your spouse would like are seasonal or if they're available year-around. Check out flowers that you may not have noticed before — something different often delights.

Pick out a good, creative florist you can talk to. It's important that he/she has the ability to figure out what your spouse would like. And in this matter your florist needs some valuable input from you. And just as having an idea or description of your spouse help you choose appropriate clothing and jewelry, so it will help you choose flowers that please.

**The Traditional Woman** She will likely have a strong streak of old-fashioned romanticism in her. She probably goes for antique furniture, flowered wallpapers and lace. She likes to wear soft silk. The flowers that are likely to please are roses, carnations, daises. An imaginative florist, armed with such information can put together an arrangement that will make you look like a hero.

**The Practical Woman** This woman likes everything she gets to last. She may not like cut flowers at all. She may want to move your gift to her garden later on. Armed with that information, the florist can make up a beautiful and endearing arrangement of flowers combined with potted green plants.

**The Exotic Spouse** Here is a woman who will likely be charmed by the unusual, the different. She may be the most difficult to choose for.

The *Marin Independent Journal*[13] suggested a list of the more exotic flowers. Check them out.

> **Anthuriums** An exotic, red, wax-like, heart-shaped, long stemmed flower that is long lasting. Often mistaken for imitation flowers.
>
> **Azaleas** These potted plants are becoming more and more popular as gift items for Valentine's Day. They provide an indoor flower show of pink or white blossoms for up to three weeks.
>
> **Bromeliads** A colorful, bright plant of the pineapple family.
>
> **Cyclamen** Cool-season potted plants, pink, red or white with lush foliage and shooting star flowers.
>
> **Hyacinths** Bulbs grown in pots indoors during winter for spring blooms in blue, white or pink. They produce a remarkable fragrance.
>
> **Freesias** Upright, tubular blossoms in red, pink, yellow, purple, orange or white, prized for their fragrance.
>
> **Proteas** These resemble pink space-age artichokes. They are used in many high-tech decorating schemes.
>
> **Ranunculus** Stand outs on their own in spring arrangements with their intense, clear colors of red, blue and white.
>
> **Strelizias** Better known as "bird of paradise" — a beautiful long-lasting, long-stemmed, exotic flower in orange with purple centers.

**Additional information about buying flowers.**

**Catalogues** Most florists have books that show pictures of floral arrangement that can be wired to other places. The drawback is two fold; they are often unimaginative, and more disappointing, what is available at the other end may not match the picture you selected.

**Flowers for Impact**   If your wallet is healthy, your lady would no doubt be delighted with bouquets of different flowers that come regularly once a month for a whole year.

**Cards**   And while you're at the florist, be sure to check out the selection of cards he has available.  (Remember we've told you that your message is very important.)  Don't have your beautiful selection accompanied by a silly card decorated with pink cupids.

**Allergies**   Be particularly careful if she is one of those who suffer from allergies to flowers.  Unfortunately, you will find out fast if you choose one that is on her list.  You might want to check this out before you buy her flowers.

**Caution**   The posies that women complained of most were the ones their spouses picked up "from a bucket" at a roadside stand on the way home or  from the local super market.  These flowers were almost unanimously unpopular.   Some said they lacked romance.   Other mentioned that they were hardly ever fresh — on their last bloom when they were brought in.

As an alternative when you are feeling spontaneous, skip the stands; think about bunches of fall leaves or budding spring branches. Try not to get arrested with this one.  Pick them where it is legal.

**A Final Tip**   Women also told us they'd much prefer you deliver the flowers in person if possible.  We suspect it's you they like to see as much as the blooms.

# 12: To Catalogue or Not

There are pros and cons concerning this next shopping suggestion — catalogue shopping. Those who have been burned by poor service, late delivery, poor quality, impersonality, and inability to touch the merchandise are extremely reluctant to use this approach or recommend it.

Others tell a different story. *Consumer Reports*[14] surveyed thousands of catalogue users and found that nine out of ten were satisfied. For them catalogues:

- Are time savers
- Give them a broader choice than they usually have in their town
- Can be used to drop hints
- Actually jog their thinking when they find them in the mail
- Ease the whole process
- Save gasoline
- Provide better help than they get in their local retail stores

Skim through a few catalogues and notice that they have personality or styles of their own, like magazines. *Sharper Image*, for example, has become known for its upscale and dramatic photos and copy. Other companies use wispy, romantic, outdoor photos and shots to sell their country-look or natural fiber clothes. Still others use fantasy-based copy in letter form or essays on product history to appeal to their customer base. Compatibility of a particular advertising style and your wife's style might even give you a clue as to whether your wife would relate to the products being sold.

## Cautions

Finally, as with any consumer activity, using catalogues to shop requires certain cautions for the buyer:

- Stick to well-established, reputable companies.

- Read product descriptions VERY carefully.

- Save the picture, description and all ordering information.

- Ask for the order taker's name.

- Ask if it is back ordered? (SKIP this gift if you are in a hurry.)

- How much delivery time? UPS or Postal Service?

- Can it be wrapped?

- What is their return policy?

- Do they pay shipping?

- Return for credit only (SKIP too complicated.)

- Don't send cash, because there is no record.

- Double check your order before you mail it in.

- Keep all shipping papers, invoices, and packing slips in case of shipping damage, wrong size, etc..

We also strongly recommend having the order shipped directly to you not to the receiver of the gift. Otherwise your partner will be put on a mailing list and soon know the price of anything you have given them.

## Simplyify Shopping

Today there are more products and specialty areas covered by catalogues than ever before. The old standards such as Spiegle, Lillian Vernon, L.L. Bean still exist. Added to this, though, are catalogues for gardeners (Smith and Hawkins), cooks (Williams Sonoma), music box collectors, silk flower arrangements, leather clothing, nature items, and many others. This diversity increases the chances of being able to find items that indicate your awareness of her interest and style.

Most large department stores such as Neiman-Marcus, Bloomingdale's, and Marshall Field's are also in the catalogue business. You can call and ask to be put on their mailing lists.

Smaller local stores have also entered this market. Watch for their catalogues in the fall as they try to hit the holiday market. These make great comparison shopping timesavers. You can call and have them hold any interesting items until you can get to the store.

Libraries even have books that can give you the names and addresses of the myriad catalogues now available. One good resource is the *New Wholesale by Mail Catalogue* usually found in the reference section of the library. *Consumer Reports (Oct. '87)* did a thorough research article on the reliability and quality of major catalogues. Check there for a recommendation of any catalogue you are uncertain about.

## A Solution for Busy Men

Since one of our premises is that it is difficult for busy men to shop, there are several aspects of catalogue shopping geared to efficiency and timesaving that we should emphasize: 800 numbers, 24-hour phones, credit cards, and computers.

The 800 numbers used now allow for faster and less expensive handling than the mail-in approach, particularly when combined with computerized stocking and ordering procedures. While you are on the line, at their expense, the retailer can check availability of your item and verify your address and phone number from the customer number on your mailing label. Using the credit card also speeds up the process since most companies wait for checks to clear before processing your order. Finally, the growing prevalence of 24-hour phone ordering extends your flexibility for shopping when it is convenient for you.

We recommend that you order early to give yourself time for an alternative choice in case you dislike the item. When your order arrives, check it carefully for damage and to see if it matches your expectations from the photo and description. When it is in front of you does it look like something that would please her? A major disadvantage to this process is, of course, not seeing the merchandise ahead of time.

If you were to have serious problems you could get assistance from

Federal Trade Commission
Pennsylvania Avenue and 6Th St. N.W.
Washington D.C.

# 13:  It's All in the Delivery

In the beginning we told you that women cherish a fantasy connected with getting a gift — a vision of how they would like the whole experience to go.  The fantasy is exaggerated, of course, but from this fantasy we can extract some of the basics of how to give a gift that will be pleasing to them.  We can also throw in some ideas on romance, dreams, and glamour to flavor your new approach.  Do remember that romance, dreams, and glamour sell.  Why else would writers such as Danielle Steele and Barbara Cartland sell millions of books with basically these same three themes?

We will start with the basics because we found that for many men their past experience had not prepared them well in this area.

Robert Masello in his article, "What Guys Don't Get About Gift Giving"[15] said, "Since wrapping, according to my father, was a waste, I automatically assumed Robin would think so too.  Since I didn't expect any little 'side dishes', I forgot that Robin might."  These side dishes — ribbons, cards, pretty paper, etc., are the significant part of PRESENTATION.

## The Basics of Presentation

- Gifts should be given on the occasion whenever possible.

- Give attention to the gift wrapping.  Don't leave the gift in the bag.

- Remove all price tags

- Use fresh, special paper and ribbon. Make use of store gift-wrapping departments if you are all thumbs, or locate your nearest paper specialty shop for boxes, paper and ribbon.

- Budget in the cost of the wrapping since custom wrapping of a present can be costly. (She may be a ribbon saver, but don't do this for her gift.)

One of the authors still remembers a Christmas early in her marriage. Her husband had taken three gifts to the gift wrapping department in an exclusive store and had them do their specialty. Three beautiful packages with unusual decorations sat under the tree for days before the unwrapping, adding to the excitement and look of the holidays. She knew the extra effort that standing in line had required, so she appreciated these packages even more. After the unwrapping, she saved the decorations for years, using them again and again, each time remembering the first time she had seen them. Although years later she has forgotten the specific gift, she still treasures the romantic wrapping.

## More Presentation Tips

- As a general rule, gifts should be personally presented. At least the giver should be there when the gift is given.

- A phone call as a present should occur early in the day or it will seem too last minute.

- Give personal items in private instead of in the midst of family or a gathering. This allows you both a chance to deal with embarrassment, should it arise, without an audience.

- Always include a personal note of any length, not just a signature, with your gift. "Love, Always, Bill" is much more meaningful than "Bill."

- This is probably a good time to remind you about the rule of NEVER asking your secretary to buy your wife's gift.

## Romantic Presentations — (Advanced Class)

Time and time again we heard from women that the ritual surrounding gift presentation was the key to a romantic gift. Most women, it seems, love the idea that you take time — LOTS of time to put a gift together. Even if all you did was purchase the gift two or three months in advance, you would be a hero. In a woman's mind this early action means you were thinking about her and caring.

This idea of Presentation is perfect for the man who loves surprises. Now you can be devious and ingenious to your heart's content as you create an experience that is fun for the receiver and the giver.

To do a first rate job with Presentation requires intuition, legwork, observation, and recognition of the receiver's uniqueness. A perfect recipe for a romantic gift.

### Examples of Romantic Presentations

Several men reported the delight their wives expressed at receiving a huge bouquet of balloons. In one case, balloons were delivered to the front door with a bottle of champagne attached along with an invitation to dinner. In another example, the delivery was made at her office, much to the delight of staff and visitors.

---

Balloons played a role in another gift as well. For his wife's 40th birthday, Tom arranged to have Laurel's office FILLED with balloons. He and two friends made special arrangements to get access to her office the night before her birthday. Then they worked feverishly, blowing up balloons and stuffing them into her office. The next morning she was greeted with a riot of colors floating in her office and the good wishes of those who had been included in the surprise.

Richard wanted to celebrate their anniversary with a cruise. He knew that this was a romantic idea, but he wanted the cruise to be extra special since it was their 10th anniversary. Months ahead of time he started bringing home brochures from different cruise lines and saying things such as, " Someday I would really like to do something like this." He listened carefully to any comments his wife made and selected the cruise she seemed most interested in. Then he bought two tickets for a cruise leaving on their anniversary. Next, he contacted their in-laws as baby sitters and swore them to secrecy. Finally, he purchased a small toy sail boat and wrote their departure date on the sail. The weekend before their anniversary, he filled their child's wading pool and took his wife out to watch his new sail boat. She read the message and looked at him in puzzlement. "That's our anniversary," she said. "I know. How would you like to be on a boat that day?" He then reached into his pocket and handed her the ticket and itinerary plus a note from her parents who had agreed to babysit. Her pleasure at the surprise and the elaborate advance work delighted them both.

Karen recalled one of the first dates with her husband Neal. He had invited her to a birthday dinner at 6:00. When she went to the door, she was met by a uniformed driver who led her to a white limousine where Neal was waiting. They drove to the San Francisco waterfront and boarded a dinner cruise boat for the evening, dining and dancing and enjoying the spectacular sunset. The same limo was waiting to drive them home.

Riley planned to give his wife, Nora, a fur coat for Christmas, but he wasn't sure about her tastes. So, he wrapped up a stuffed animal wearing a fake fur jacket and holding a scroll. On the scroll was written, "I.O.U. one fur coat of your choosing to be selected by you on an outing on a date of your choice between Dec. 26 and Jan. 4." Nora was pleased with his creativity, the time they would spend together, and the clever presentation she could share with her friends.

> Mary Kay Ash, the founder of the successful Mary Kay Cosmetics firm, told us a story about her husband and romantic gift giving. "We were married on a Thursday. In the following week, in celebration of our 'first anniversary' Mel brought me a lovely gift. I was so surprised and responded by saying . 'Oh, my goodness, this is wonderful. Are you going to do this every week?' Sure enough the following Thursday another gift complete with a rose and a card was in my dressing room. He continued to do this every single Thursday for 14 years until his death. He always said that he wanted to keep the romance alive in our marriage, and he did."

**Does being romantic or creating a fantasy have to be expensive and always require so much prep time? No.**

**Feasible Fantasies:**

- Sometimes the romance can come from lighting a candle or putting a fire in the fireplace just before you present the gift.

- Sometimes it can be achieved by tracking down some small item she admired and had given up ever having.

- Sometimes it can be created by tying a beautiful silk ribbon around a shiny white box.

- A spontaneous romantic gift might be a "fireplace picnic" kit. Pack together a small package of kindling, perfumed candles, favorite wine, cheese, and crackers. This kit could be used at home or as the invitation to a run-away weekend.

- A simple romantic gift involves making a tape of her or your mutual favorite music.

- Marking your personal milestones is one of the best ways to be romantic.

- Observing wedding anniversaries is an important romantic ritual. But consider something novel, such as celebrating the anniversary of your first date, or the day you got engaged, or the day you moved into your first house.

- You might even go a step further and recreate your first date.

- To celebrate an engagement anniversary, you could talk about or write about the reasons you originally chose each other. To mark a house anniversary, spend some time discussing what the house means to your life together.

**A romantic gift** should not be generic. It is important to have the recipient in mind. This is not the time to give a predictable gift.

Recently the *Bill Cosby Show* approached the problem of gifts and romance. The three husbands on the show challenged each other to find the most romantic gift without spending more than $25 plus tax for their wives. In the first case, the son-in-law gave his wife the first pearl of a long wished-for pearl necklace.

The second son-in-law presented his wife with the handkerchief he'd used to wipe off her lipstick the first time they had kissed and a flower from her wedding bouquet. Both items were to be put into a small container and buried as a time capsule in their first home's backyard. They were to dig it up on significant anniversaries and remember their feelings at the time of these two events. (Few of us are far sighted enough to have kept this sort of thing, but start thinking ahead now. There are tenth anniversaries to remember, the birth of a children, even grandchildren. Save a momento.)

Finally, Bill's character presented his wife with a plastic bracelet she had admired when they were dating in high school. At that time he could not afford to buy it for her. Now, he had contacted antique collectable dealers to help him with his search. Each of these gifts was accompanied by a short, loving statement of the men's feelings of present love, past memories and future plans — the equation for romance and dreams.

In summary, just remember what one of our interviewees said, "presentation is half the giving process." Putting thought into the presentation is *Langnappe* — a New Orleans word that means "just a little something extra". Presentation is an elegant way of saying you thought about her, the KEY to all successful giving.

# 14: Putting It In Writing

*There are few satisfactions in life that can compare with the knowledge that you have obtained some mastery over words.*

*Melvin H. Miller*

---

Something was wrong. Nat was puzzled by Marcia's response. He had been so pleased with himself; he had actually remembered a silk scarf Marcia had admired on a recent shopping expedition and had found it still in stock a few days later when he returned to buy it for a "congratulations on your promotion" present. Yet, her response was reserved and a bit withdrawn.

"Isn't this the one you liked?"

"Oh, yes, it is the right one. Thank you for remembering." Long, uncomfortable pause. "I was just wishing you had written a note or put in a card." There was no joy in Mudville that day either.

The men we talked to said they agreed in principle to the idea of a note or card, but that it was in this area that they most often slacked off. They said that since cards didn't mean much to them, they assumed others felt the same. <u>Not True</u>.

Even we were surprised at how often women mentioned that they saved all written correspondence, particularly notes on cards they received. They treasured these personal communications long after the event. Even the woman who throws out everything is likely to keep anything written by you.

---

### Basic Guidelines to Note Writing

1. Use good off-white or gray paper, and black or blue ink. (In reality, pencil or scratch paper will be accepted, but we are trying for romantic flair here.)

2. Don't fret about grammar, spelling or punctuation. This could just stop you from saying something special.

3. Focus on your feelings not just your thoughts.

4. Images are a useful technique. Use examples from nature or life experiences you have shared such as movies or books. (Of course, her hair isn't golden threads, but take poetic license. You feel it reminds you of golden threads, or liquid onyx. Use this image.)

---

**If you are having trouble getting started:**

- First write a list of 10 things you appreciate about her. You now have either 10 separate notes, or the start of a poem, or a guideline for expanding and elaborating your thoughts.

- Browse a card shop's selection of romantic cards. These people know their business. Pick the card that expresses the words you wished you had thought of. Write that wish on the card and present it to her.

- Look at ads for inspiration. Again you are dealing with the masters. Here are some phrases we found and adapted that might help you trigger your personal note:

"A rose for each year we have shared."

"This color blue always reminds me of your eyes."

"You share your humorous side, lucky me."

Brenda Shapiro in her *Chicago* magazine article, "Between Friends and Lovers"[16] recounted this inspiring example." Her husband gave her a superb strand of real pearls for their anniversary, but she, a writer, mentions them not for what the oysters wrought, but for his elegant note.

---

J____,

           Flawless in every way, the first 35.

                  Love, _____ "

---

Don't be afraid to attempt lengthier notes.  Here are some examples:

> If I promise to make reservations for dinner on Valentine's Day, will you promise to wear these new earrings with your red dress that always seduces me?

> I must have been missing you.  Everything reminded me of you.  The faint hint of perfume in the cab I grabbed said, "you." So I stopped to buy you a bottle.  I always want this to remind me of you.

> To my very special jewel.  More precious to me than all of the other kind together.

For the truly inspired or brave, there is always the POEM!

What! You say, "I can't. Impossible!" If you can write a business letter, a memo, a clear note to the car mechanic, you CAN do it. Make it easier by setting the words to a well-known song, maybe even "your " song. It is okay if your poem sounds a bit ragged or the rhyme is off. She will treasure the effort.

Go the extra mile. Give the extra touch. A note says you took the TIME and that "you cared enough to send the very best," (says Hallmark). Her memory of your caring will last a long time.

# 15: Valentine's Day

We agree with the many of you who feel that there is something out of whack about Valentine's Day in this country. Somehow a simple day has become burdened with the task of proving love, caring and devotion to another — all in one day and with one magic gift. It has become a day of disappointment, embarrassment and pressure.

There is nothing wrong with the concept of a day to be thoughtful and loving to our spouse. We just object to the idea that husbands and wives are being coerced and pressured into exaggerated responses.

So how do you go about changing this state of affairs?

Well, we don't recommend a diatribe on the commercialization of holidays and the triteness of certain cards and decorations. That will just make you seem pompous and perhaps a little cheap.

The odds are she has similar feelings. So how about starting with a calm and gentle talk with her about how you, as a couple, might chose to make it a loving day? Ask her what would please her; tell her what would please you. Be sure you don't lock in a script. Leave some room for playfulness, spontaneity and creativity.

Remember that despite the barrage of advertising, most women told us two important things about Valentine's Day:

- They didn't expect or require an extravagant gift.
  Remembrance was the real issue.

● It was not necessary for this year's gift to be bigger, more expensive, more elaborate than last year's.

We found *Esquire Etiquette*[17] to have some suggestions that were romantic, but not cloying — a tough balance to achieve. We are pleased to share some of their ideas with you to get you started.

"The question, then, is not <u>whether</u> to acknowledge Valentine's Day, but <u>how</u> to acknowledge it with grace and flair and a modicum of dignity."

---

### Valentine Winners

1. A perfect rose served with fresh morning coffee and freshly squeezed orange juice delivered to her on a tray.

2. Dinner at an embarrassingly romantic restaurant where you can actually hold hands.

3. A brief note written on just about anything EXCEPT a Valentine's Day card.

4. A distinctive, but not breathtakingly expensive gift. Something decidedly personal (ie. not a toaster oven) and not candy.

---

And if you happen to be out of town? Leave a "to be opened on Valentine's Day" card or note. Call her last thing at night and tell her she is still your Valentine. Leave clues to lead her to figure out where you will go for dinner when you get back.

In general, this is a wonderful time to be creative and develop something meaningful for just the two of you. This may be the night you rent the most romantic movie you can find, light a fire in the fireplace, and snuggle. Make it a day for lovers, not just a charge account attack.

# 16:  The Gift of Time with You

This Gift of Your Time is what women tell us they want more than anything.  It's the cheapest and yet the most expensive gift you can give her.  We know you are often under great pressure and time to play is often unfortunately measured in teaspoons. She knows that too, which is why she will cherish attention lavished upon her even if it must sometimes be brief.   So throughout this book there are examples of great gifts that are special primarily because they include Time Together.

This might be the time to suggest:

> 1. Agree to share some task — paint the kitchen?  dig up the tulip bulbs?
>
> 2. Promise to go antique hunting some Sunday afternoon.
>
> 3. Plan a monthly Saturday date for the two of you.
>
> 4. Take an early morning or late afternoon walk together several times a week.

Just concentrate on the small stuff.  Time together doesn't have to mean a cruise, although....

# 17:  For List Lovers

*Watch your step when you know immediately the one way to do anything.  Nine time out of ten, there are several better ways.*

*William B Given Jr.*

---

Some people like lists; they get inspired by lists. If you're one of these, the following might be right up your alley.

# How to Find Romance Where You Live

Do you need to jump-start your imagination when it comes to ideas for romance? Here's a listing from "CALIFORNIA ROMANCE, WHERE TO FIND IT" from *WW*[18] to get you started. We have tried to show that these ideas can be put to use wherever you live.

**A bouquet of violets from a flower stall on the San Francisco streets**
Violets grow everywhere.

**Tea at the Hotel Bel-Air**
Call the biggest hotel in town and ask them if they serve tea.

**Fisherman's Wharf on a rainy day in the off-season**
Rainy day walks with a big umbrella anywhere.

**Being serenaded by mariachis**
How about an accordion player from your local Elks Club?

**Strolling along the rugged coast at Point Lobos**
Nearly every place has a remote place.

**Walking through the poppy fields outside Lancaster**
Find your local arboretum.

**Buying armfuls of flowers early in the morning at the Los Angeles flower mart**
The secret of this is "an armload."

**Early morning cappuccino at one of the little Italian cafes in San Francisco's North Beach area**

You could ask to reserve a booth at your local cafe. It's the idea that counts.

**Riding horses through the surf on a deserted beach on the Sonoma Coast in Northern California**
You don't have a horse? How about a bicycle?

**Tea-dancing in the Peacock Room at the Mark Hopkins Hotel**
It's the nostalgia we're suggesting here.

**Picking wild strawberries on the Mendocino Coast**
You may not have a coast, but every place has berries.

**Sailing on San Francisco Bay**
Sailing anywhere.

**Playing hide and seek in the boxwood hedges in the garden of the Filoli estate in Woodside**
Figure this one out on your own.

**Whale-watching from the cliffs of Palos Verdes**
No whales? Try the aquarium.

**Amber House, the bed and breakfast hotel in Sacramento**
Fortunately bed and breakfasts are springing up everywhere.

**Strolling through the farmer's market in San Luis Obispo**
Women tell us that open markets early in the morning are very romantic places.

**Taking a catamaran to Catalina Island and landing at a deserted beach**
The key is the deserted beach or meadow or field or woods.

**Bike-riding at sunset between Marina del Rey and Manhattan Beach**
Any sunset bike ride has an element of romance.

**Searching for spring wild flowers in the deserted canyons of the Mojave**
Wild flowers are lovely anywhere.

**Riding the ferris wheel overlooking the bay at Newport Beach**
Ferris wheels, merry-go-rounds, even porch swings make you
feel young and carefree.

**Camping at Tuolumne Meadows in Yosemite**
Camping has special appeal in the moonlight.

**Tandem bike riding anywhere**

**The East Brother Lighthouse, East Brother Island, San
Francisco Bay — accessible only by private launch**
Look around for something different where you are.

**Jogging early morning over the Golden Gate Bridge**
Early morning jogs or walks make you feel good.

**Walking through the mists in Redwood National Park**
Parks and gardens are particularly appealing in the mist.

**Kissing in an opera box at the San Francisco Opera**
You don't have to kiss, but it's not a bad idea.

**Exploring ghost towns in the Mother Lodge country**
Old towns have a special appeal.

Almost **anything** can be made romantic for your spouse if **you**
initiate it.

# Anniversary Code

Traditionally, wedding anniversaries are associated with certain gifts. Here are some ideas for each category drawn from many sources. It is more important, in the long run, to select something appropriate to her wants.

| YEAR | SYMBOL | GIFT IDEAS |
| --- | --- | --- |
| 1 | Paper | subscriptions, cookbook, stationary, photo albums, tickets, gift certificates, coupons for special favors |
| 2 | Cotton | matching tee-shirts, cotton hammock, quilt, Swiss handkerchief |
| 3 | Leather | real leather photo album or frame, briefcase, wallet, driving gloves |
| 4 | Silk/ Flowers | silk flowers, rose bush, silk pillow cases |
| 5 | Silverware/ Wood | bookends, trinket box, music box, tree for the yard pendant, thimble, bookmark, dresser set, bangle bracelets |
| 6 | Iron | travel iron, book ends |
| 7 | Wool | sweater, scarf, stadium blanket, soft afghan |
| 8 | Bronze/ Pottery/ Linen or Lace | wind chimes, garden sculpture, large pitcher for wild flowers ingerie, lace trimmed pillows, down comforter and duvet in Belgium lace |

| | | |
|---|---|---|
| 9 | Pottery/ Willow | Cachepots for plants, breakfast set for two, blue willow pattern dishes, wicker bed tray |
| 10 | Tin/ Aluminum | tintype, cookie cutters, tennis racquet, bike, antique kitchen utensils |
| 11 | Steel | this one is tough — a car? |
| 12 | Pearls | Jewelry, inlaid box |
| 15 | Crystal | punch bowl, crystal handled make-up brushes, hand mirror, paperweight, dressing table set, two goblets |
| 20 | China | figurines |
| 30 | Diamond | self-explanatory |
| 35 | Coral/ Jade | perhaps a trip to Hong Kong or Hawaii to purchase some jewelry |
| 40 | Ruby | see if she likes these stones first |
| 45 | Sapphire | anniversary guard ring |
| 50 | Gold | you are on your own by this time |

# Idea Jogger

After all the ideas you have read about, maybe you could use a short, simple starter list as an idea jogger. Once you start thinking, add to the list with your own ideas.

**For the Hobbyist**
subscription to the appropriate hobby magazine
special scissors (sewing, gardening, crafts, etc.)

**For the Collector**
display shelf or cabinet
shadow box

**For the Artist**
easel
top quality brushes
kiln

**For the Gardening Buff**
books on flower or vegetable gardening secrets
vases of different sizes

**For the Fitness Buff**
jumprope
pedometer
tote bag

**For the Business Woman**
attache case
name plate
letter opener
card case

**For the History Buff**
framed family tree
biography

**For the Music Lover**
piano lamp
concert tickets

# One Survey Says[19]

| What do Women Want? | What Don't Women Want? |
| --- | --- |
| Leather goods | Shoes |
| Silk nightclothes | Office supplies |
| Framed photographs | Household appliances |
| Her favorite movie on cassette | A season subscription to |
| A week-end away | something you figure she'll |
| Perfume | go to with the girls |
| Flowers | Alcohol |
| A housekeeper | Surprise pets |
| Pearls | Cooking classes |
| A night in a hotel | Strippers/singing telegrams |
| A break from the kids | Gift Certificates |

# 18: The Last Minute Solution — For His Eyes Only

THE SCENARIO: You're on overload — too much to do. In the back of your mind you know you've needed to get an important gift for an important time for her. You didn't get it done. It's now the witching hour and you're up against it. There's no time to purchase any of the items that crossed your mind during your busy meetings. You know she's expecting something special. You feel a panic attack. Some of the ideas below are elsewhere in this book, but this is no time for study.

## Immediate Solutions to Save You

1.  Go to a well known jeweler and buy an interesting stone — one that shows off her eyes or her personality. Have the jeweler wrap it beautifully . Put in a note telling her you'd like to discuss the design for the settling. Or, tell her she's good at design and you wanted her to design it herself in just the way she likes.

2.  Is there someone at work who can draw? Have him/her draw a vision of a romantic trip — an island, a ship, if it's big time; a charming bed and breakfast if it's a week-end you have in mind. Put her name on it — and maybe your name too. Call your travel agent. Book a trip. Roll the art work into a scroll, tie it up and present it to her.

3.  You have a few more minutes? Pick up the tickets from the travel agent. Drop by a drug store and pick up a pretty cosmetic

travel kit and tuck the tickets inside. If you've chosen a cruise, give her the tickets in a toy boat.

4. Pick up a lavish romance novel, some bubble bath and scurry her off to soak and read while you take care of the kids.

5. Buy a dozen longstemmed red roses. Pick up two tickets to the ballet or the symphone or whatever is coming to town, and tuck them among the flowers.

6. On a budget? Movie tickets work too and you an get to your local theatre on your way home. Ask them what's going to be playing and pick out a romantic movie to add to the note you will write. Put it in a box of popcorn.

7. Give her a gift certificate to an antique shop. Put the certificate and your note in a skein of yarn.

8. Call a good deli. Get a gift certificate for a big basket to be delivered for a party. The date is her choice. She'll be the hostess. Put your certificate in a small basket with champagne and nibbles.

9. Or put an invitation for dinner at an Italian restaurant into a box of spaghetti.

10. Pick up candles to float in the bathtub — add your favorite tape.

11. Drop by your super market and pick up an exotic fruit, maybe a pomegranate. Add a note with a promise of passion.

12. Create an I.O.U. coupon on your computer. Make sure it's for something good. As the *Wall Street Journal* puts it, an, "I.O.U a diamond is not the same as when you were a child and gave your mother an 'I.O.U one vacuuming.' " No computer? Hand written is even better.

13. Call in a reservation for a candlelight dinner for two at a romantic restaurant. Drop by the restaurant and pick up the menu (most restaurants will let you have it) and wrap the menu as the gift. No time? Many cities have reasonable priced

messenger services. (Those kids who expertly cut in and out of traffic on their bikes. Put them to work.)

14. Even a convenience store like 7-Eleven had possibilities. Pick up a couple of soft drinks, and candy bars for a romantic "picnic on a blanket."

# 19:  Better Yet, Think Ahead

*The best way to escape from a problem is to solve it.*
*Brendan Francis*

---

We've never yet met a wife who really likes a last minute gift. You can hand her a Tiffany Egg, but if she knows you've dashed out to buy it on the day of the event, it might as well be a hunk of mackerel. Buying ahead shows you care. (It also keeps that desperate feeling at bay.)

This can be easy if you stay alert. *Esquire* puts it well, "Say you and your wife are strolling through a crafts fair at midsummer, and she falls seriously in love with a hand-carved jewelry box. Her birthday was last month, and your anniversary isn't until October. What's a thoughtful, loving husband to do? Figure out a way to buy the box without her knowing it, that's what."

It's a wise idea always to have some small gift in the larder, just like an insurance policy. And having lovingly worded cards stashed away is equally stress reducing. Does that mean you have to think gifts all the time? Quite the contrary. Acquiring the habit of buying-when-you-see-it gives you the leeway to be spontaneous when it is gifting time.

Stashing ahead also prepares you for an emergency. Problems do happen that can make you forget your own name, let alone your anniversary. Just about anywhere you live you can find immediate delivery services — flowers, candy, balloons. Keep a listing of telephone numbers. With these numbers you are well armed for any occasion. So if some morning you wake up with a lady who is humming the birthday song to herself, you can roll over secure in the knowledge that you have situation well in hand. No problem.

# 20: Talk It Over

*To talk to someone who does not listen is enough to tense the devil.*

*Pearl Bailey*

---

Nothing beats direct communication for cutting through old gift customs and misconceptions. Once you've explored your half of this book, and hopefully, your spouse has done the same, we suggest you discuss it with each other. A good discussion could save years of confusion.

What's the best way to start talking you ask? As you can imagine, accusations, challenges, or analysis will get you nowhere. Since the point is to open up communication our advice is simple:

**TRY:**

> "I would enjoy hearing your reactions to..."
>
> "Were there any surprises for you?"
>
> "I came to realize something while I was reading and wanted to tell you..."
>
> Use the questions from Chapter 3

**AVOID:**

> "Why don't you ever..."
>
> "You never..."
>
> "Now I know what's wrong. Why you always..."

Good wishes for a good discussion.

# For Her

# 21: Behind the Gift Story

Wives love to get presents from their husbands. A gift that truly delights, enhances the whole relationship and makes everybody happy.

What we've discovered, however, is that it can be very difficult for your spouse to give you a gift that really hits the mark.

Our object is to make sure that from now on his gift to you will be cause for a happy time, one you both look forward to with great pleasure.

Now pay attention: More than half this book was written "for his eyes only" as a guide for him to make it easy to know what you like. Since this section was written for him, not for you, the language and comments are directed to him. If you would rather not read about your next gift, then skip that portion. If you prefer to check what we are telling him, read away.

But you don't get off that easy. You may have hidden agendas and expectations that complicate what should be a simple matter. As we interviewed women, we came to realize that you need to understand your half of the equation. Nothing is one sided. Let's take a look at your part of the book.

# 22: Unwrapping the Family Patterns

We all come into our relationships with certain expectations — many arising from the customs and patterns we experienced growing up. It was clear from our very first interview that families differed widely in their gift giving practices — from an all out elaborate extravagance for, say an anniversary, to ignoring the event completely.

We expected that couples accustomed to similar gifting styles in their families would have a much easier time with any gift problems. This proved to be exactly the case. But most of us aren't so lucky. Many of us married men whose patterns don't match what we're used to at all.

Since family gatherings and celebrations are more likely to fall into our bailiwick, our customs, rather than his, are more likely to be the ones followed. This is especially true if we have some very strong opinion about such things. Men told us they often had customs of their own that they would like to repeat, but they went along with their spouses' patterns because it was just easier. Conrad told us, for example, that his family celebrated every holiday on the books, even May Day — a time when his father traditionally hung a big basket of fresh flowers on the front door. When he married his wife, who came from a family where only Christmas and anniversaries were celebrated, she was astounded when Conrad began making elaborate May Day plans. But she found she liked to celebrate and from then on copied Conrad's family traditions.

Recognizing the vast differences in family customs can be a great help to you — and a great relief. With recognition you can move on from a very sensitive issue where feelings can be bruised to an opportunity to look at the bigger picture. Even better, this understanding gives you and your spouse a smorgasbord from which you can choose your own gifting patterns.

Understanding the patterns and customs (and therefore the limitations) we bring with us to our relationships is so important that we've reviewed this subject more thoroughly in the men's section. The men we interviewed felt strongly that a good discussion with their wives to review their customs and expectations would help immensely. The sooner the better!

# 23: Thanks, I Think

You may never have given it a thought, but there is an art to receiving a gift and many of us are not very good at it. Much of your response may have come from the family patterns you adopted early on, so you may want to do some soul searching. How **do** you respond when he gives you a gift one, let's say, that really delights you in every way? It certainly surprised us to discover that many women aren't very skilled at showing their appreciation, let alone responding with enthusiasm and excitement. It was confirmed when some men told us things like, "I think she was really pleased, but I can't tell for sure." Why is it, then, that it's so difficult for some of us to express our pleasure?

One woman told us, "I didn't show my real pleasure even though I loved the present. As I was growing up, my family was never very demonstrative. I was carefully taught not to show my emotions." Most of us learned the basic, "Say, 'thank you,' to Aunt Lucy." These perfunctory rules of gift etiquette left us unprepared for more legitimate and enthusiastic responses. These phrases set a pattern of response for many of us: obligatory, restrained, flat.

Another piece of early training taught us what to do when we got a book that was "good for us" instead of the fun toy we had our heart set on; or we got practical mittens when we longed for a diary with a key. And yet we were often required to be appreciative. We all learned well how to be restrained in our responses, since enthusiasm might result in the same gift next year. And to make it all the more uncomfortable, there was always that dreaded duty of having to write a note for something you never really wanted in the first place.  Such training teaches **Caution.**

Or you may have grown up in a family that felt it was too materialistic or too worldly to focus on gifts much less to exclaim over them.  You may have seen only very low-keyed responses such as mild nods or comments such as, "This will come in handy," or, "You shouldn't have bothered."  You may never have witnessed any examples of full blown enthusiasm and excitement.

No doubt about it, these early experiences still color your responses today.

As adults you may have picked up a "thank you" style that cames from trial and error, generally based on learning to be polite and pleasing others.  This style is usually at least acceptable, perhaps even effusive in some cases.  Unfortunately, these learned patterns can also add to our confusion.  Without a genuine, heartfelt response, you can lose touch with what is real, what you really appreciate.  Janet S. reported, "I sometimes feel so artificial, even phony when I go what I call 'overboard' praising my husband's gift to me.  Telling him how wonderful he was just to have remembered.  I feel that I remember everyone in the family, and no one ever seems to notice this.  It all seems out of whack."

Showing appreciation and giving praise are activities that get passed over often in our fast-paced society.  Men respond to praise just like women do, and most especially, they need positive reinforcement when they've picked out an important gift.  It's very important to your relationship to let him know that his gift means a great deal to you.  No matter how competent he is, or how matter-of-fact he appears (some men get very good at this) he has **feelings**.  He doesn't like rejection any more than you do.  Yet, we were surprised at how difficult it is for many women to express their delight and show their enthusiasm.

Just how do you go about showing enthusiasm when you haven't had much practice?  You may want to memorize some of the following responses and act them out until they come naturally:

- Stand up and hug him for your gift. A kiss isn't a bad idea either.

- Look him in the eye when you say thank you. <u>Smile warmly</u>.

- Take the time to really thank him, to show your appreciation — don't rush right on to something else. Timing is so important that you may want to set the scene for any exchange of gifts — a quiet restaurant, for example, some place that gives you a break from the family.

- Try it on immediately, if it's wearable. Show him how great it looks.

  Margy's Christmas gift was beautiful emerald stud earrings. She immediately changed into a white suit with a green blouse to show off the special gift and wore that suit all day long to let him how how well he had chosen.

- Say some positive phrases: Such as, "Hey, this is really great," or, "How did you know I'd love this?" Men told us some spouses seemed tongue-tied. Don't be at a loss for words — speak up and tell him how much you appreciate his gift.

# 24: What Myths Are You Into?

Old myths are a part of the equation too. Let's take a look at some old myths that may be interfering with your enjoyment. When it comes to him buying you a gift, there are some pervasive myths that abound that need to be examined.

## MYTH ONE "If He Really Loves Me, He'll Know Just What I Want."

It would be hard to estimate the untold damage this myth has done to anniversary dinners, Christmas mornings and birthday celebrations. Yet some of us cherish the belief that magically knowing what we would like equals being loved. "I don't expect her to know intuitively what I want," one man told us, "so why would she think I would know exactly what she wants".

**On re-examining this myth:** Chances are that you think a lot about gifts; it's almost as if it's ingrained in the female species. Men aren't likely to think about gifts in the same absorbed, detailed way that women do. Have you ever spotted something beautiful in a store window — and walked by again and again imagining all the places that gift might take you? If you have a good imagination, there's no limit to what you can think up. Maybe what you saw was a turquoise necklace. Think how he'd like it over candlelight on your new black velvet dress. And wouldn't it look stunning with a white tank top in the summer when you have a tan? The interesting point is this type of "dreaming away" is foreign territory to most men. Some men manage, you've noticed, to do pretty well at Eddie Bauer's or at a good hardware store. "Since men are not even dimly aware of what's available in the marketplace," writes Warren Leight for *Mademoiselle*, "they do not know what there is to want." That lack of knowledge has little to do with loving; it has everything to do with differences in thinking patterns. So, unless you let him know in some way, there isn't a ghost of a chance he'll be buying you that coveted turquoise necklace. The good news is that once this myth has been scrutinized and understood for what it is, you can take some positive action. Think of what a relief it will be not to feel that pang of disappointment as you open your gift on your next big anniversary. It's up to you. Think about it. If this myth is in your way, it's worth making a change so you'll feel good.

## MYTH TWO  "If I Have to Tell Him What I Want, It Doesn't Count."

This really is Part 2 of the "If he loves me, he'll know" myth above. Somehow there's a widespread belief that the gift he gives doesn't count as much if we have to tell him. In interviewing women this was often a very sensitive issue. When asked, "What would you like for your birthday?" women often admitted to saying, "Oh, just anything." Do we still have a distorted vision that he should always be all-knowing, including what we want as a gift? Is it that we've been trained to believe it isn't lady-like to say what we really want? Do we think of it as selfish?

**On re-examining:** It really doesn't matter what the reasons are for being hung up on this myth. What counts is that it can cause many unhappy and confusing times. Men tell us this myth puts them behind the eight-ball. They are frustrated by our response of, "Oh, anything's fine." Remember men aren't likely to ask what you want if they don't really want to know. Do you want your husband to think that you really have no idea what you want? By the way, we're not suggesting that all men ask. If you have one that does, consider yourself lucky. If you want to know our specifics on how to tell him what you want — move right ahead to Chapter 22. For now, we want you to take a long hard look at this myth and see if it's worth the discomfort it may be causing you and your husband.

## MYTH THREE "His Gift Must Be a Surprise."

Where did this irrational idea originate? We don't know either. But many women told us that only a surprise counted as "a real present." Men told us this myth was often perplexing to them.

**On re-examining:** Certainly our society encourages the idea that gifts and surprises are synonymous. Take Christmas. All those presents under the tree wrapped to hide the contents, enticing the recipient by camouflaging, puzzling and teasing. This can be a fun game that can last for weeks before the Big Day, adding to the excitement of the whole event.

But it isn't the only game in town. And gift giving, as we've noted again and again in this book, can be risky business if the surprise misses.

If you are one who has always thought that he must surprise you with every gift, then you may want to know what some other people do. Men have told us that some of their most successful gifts were not surprises. Nick reported that he asked his wife to reserve one Friday afternoon around their anniversary. They would have lunch together and then go to the nursery to pick out several colorful bouganvilla plants to go in front of their house — something she had mentioned several times. After brunch they went home and put the new plants in the ground. On their anniversary, he gave her a card and she set up a picnic table in front of the new plants. With candles.

Sam did a version of this for their 10th anniversary. On their afternoon together, they went to the jewelry store to choose a gold anniversary band. He then presented his wife with the ring (engraved and all) on their anniversary. She's still talking about it.

**In conclusion** Although surprises can be great fun, there are other very satisfying alternatives. Why limit yourself?

# 25: Disappointments Are Not Healthy

*All problems become smaller if you don't dodge*
*them, but confront them. Touch a thistle timidly, and*
*it pricks you; grasp it boldly, and its spines crumble.*
*William S. Halsey*

---

Gifts are meant to make others happy so it's really a let-down to have any gift create disappointment. Yet in our interviews, we seldom encountered a woman who had not felt disappointed at one time or another with an important gift from her partner. But the ways in which the women handled that disappointment ran the whole gamut from complete honesty to a highly developed version of play acting.

We certainly don't have all the answers on how honest to be about your gift disappointments, but we thought you'd want to know how other women deal with this very sensitive subject.

## Ways in Which Women Handled Their Disappointments

### She's Honest and Open, but Gentle

Yvonne told us that her first big gift disappointment came very early in their relationship. He proposed and gave her a surprise engagement ring. To her the guy was wonderful; the ring was not. So she told him that she loved him and wanted to spend the rest of her life with him — but not with the ring. She asked that they return it together and select another. They did. And the last time we saw them they were indeed living happily ever after.

Yvonne noted that all other aspects of their relationship had always been open and honest, so gift giving had to be treated in the same vein. Open, honest, but loving.

**Observation** This seemed very healthy to us. The earlier in the relationship you share total honesty and trust, the better. But we know this doesn't work for every couple.

### She's Completely Honest, No Matter What

A few women responded to a disappointing gift very directly. Some people would say they are brutally honest. "How could you think I'd like this? You know I hate purple. And this sweater is not my style."

**Observation** There certainly is no room for misunderstanding here. But this method doesn't seem very promising for long-term, positive, gift-getting results.

### She's Diplomatically Honest

A larger number of women told us they let their husbands know their true feelings about a gift that missed — but they did it with great care. They timed their response carefully. They first praised him for his thoughtfulness and caring and the time he had spent, then told him they'd like to exchange it for another color, size, gift or whatever, and would he mind. Like Yvonne, they often asked that he go with them.

**Observation** This seems to work well for many people. It says you trust he has a healthy ego.

### She's Protecting His Feelings. It's Her First Priority

Alice Mulligan has been married for nearly fifty years and has eight grandchildren. She reports that she has always "put on a show" over any present her husband buys her. Most of his gifts are ones that she would never have chosen for herself. He leans toward the glitzy-gaudy, especially in jewelry, and her choice would be far more conservative. But she wears his presents and basks in the pleasure he gets from seeing his gift displayed. Not for the world would she tell him her real feelings or exchange his selection.

**Observation** This is a matter of priorities. She has adjusted well and built a pattern over the years that works for her. Many women we talked to used to respond in this way, but can no longer do it as well. Perhaps the consciousness raising of the women's movement has changed their old patterns as they confront how they really feel.

Here is another example. Allyson also places her husband's feelings high on her priority list. She's been married a couple of years and just has had their first child. She's the keeper of the family's finances so she knows where the money goes. When her son was born her husband gifted her with a pair of diamond stud earrings, "one from me and one from our son." She was delighted. He is a very busy man right now and that thoughtfulness gave her great joy. But she felt some disappointment too. The earrings were within the budget a starting family could afford, therefore they were very small. Allyson has a friend in the wholesale jewelry business where the size of the diamonds could be doubled at the same price. But, Allyson told us, she didn't have the heart to tell him.

**Observation** This is a touchy situation and we empathize. Allyson is not like Alice Mulligan. Her personal preference is very important to her and no set patterns have yet been established. As an alternative, Allyson might have said, "I can't believe you found the time to buy this wonderful gift. I feel guilty bringing this up, but I know you'd want me to. Our friend Betty knows the wholesale jewelry mart and knows where we can get a really good bargain. Would you mind if we doubled the size of those wonderful earrings at the same price?" This might be the kindest thing to do in the long run. He'll notice if she's not wearing those earrings, and she'll never be quite satisfied otherwise.

### She's Play-acting but Resenting It

Martha Jane admits she put on a pretense for years. Hers is also a long marriage. And a good marriage. He is a professional athlete and sees her as a fine homemaker which she is and enjoys being, but she also longs for affirmation of her other talents. His gifts don't make her feel happy or loved. His major presents have included a very high tech sewing machine, (she hates to sew), the most elaborate Cuisinart, (she's a simple cook) and even a vacuum cleaner. Top of the line. She loves him, but over the years has piled up resentments over these "not me" gifts as she calls them. She longs for the personal touch, such as jewelry or feminine lingerie. She wishes she knew how to tell him.

**Observation**  Resentments have a way of building up until they pop out in other forms. Her crying spells around Christmas time, for example, are a puzzlement to him. She might want to try one of the other approaches we have presented.

### She Responds to Disappointments With Little White Lies

Many women reported that they had developed sly ways of "saving his ego" by praising his gift lavishly, if not honestly, and exchanging it at the first opportunity. "A little white lie never hurt anyone," one woman responded, "and it makes him feel good. I'll just exchange it for what I want. He'll never know and we'll both be happy."

**Observation**  There's no doubt that this is a common practice — as the exchanges at the department store the day after Christmas would attest. But, we admit, we aren't completely comfortable with this solution. We may have been the only two people in the USA that found the old *I Love Lucy* TV shows uncomfortable. That famous format of Lucy's — I'll-do-what-I-want-and-hide-it-from-Ricky-since-he-won't-approve always ended the same when he discovered her ruse and forgave her. That produced good comedy and maybe was good practice for the 1950's. But we prefer the thinking of the 1990's and more open relationships between men and women.

### She Goes Silent Because She Thinks His Gift Is Telling Her to Change

Some women told us they felt his gift was trying to tell her he was not pleased with who she was. Ruth, who is age 60 and on the round side, received a black lace teddy, two sizes too small. Two years ago her husband gave her a rowing machine. These presents carry a double disappointment — she longed and hinted for new additions to her silver bracelet collection and she feels he's telling her something she doesn't want to hear — that she isn't as attractive as she used to be.

**Observation** This situation calls for a good talk not silence. We keep stressing the need for good communication. The problem might be that he's not in such good shape himself. Men often think of their spouses as being smaller than they are and aren't very good at remembering sizes. A local newspaper ran a story a couple of years ago regarding the perception men and women have of each other's weight. Most women think that they are a few pounds overweight and their spouse would like them slimmer. Most men, on the contrary, thought their spouse just right. (Ironically, most men are overweight according to the charts, but think themselves about the right size , and most women would like a slimmer spouse.)

### She Turns the Disappointment Around by Recognizing the Possibilities of the Gift

Marla's gift, an unusual dramatic necklace, although beautiful, was a disappointment to her. At first. It wasn't at all what she expected or what she usually wore with her mostly casual California look. She then realized that the problem wasn't the gift, but, rather, that she needed to be a little creative — get out of her rut. The gift called for a simple top she didn't have. Once she got it worked out, that necklace became her favorite piece.

**Observation** Sometimes we get caught in a rut, and a gift that shows a new perspective can be a real pick-me-up. Such a present can add a new dimension to your life. It can encourage you to expand a little, to break away from an old pattern that may have become a habit  One woman we interviewed told us about the time her husband gave her an expensive swimming mask for her birthday. It was a big disappointment — she had her heart set on an antique evening bag. This woman had never been much of a swimmer because she always disliked putting her face in the water. Her husband insisted she give the gift a try. Now she wouldn't trade that mask for anything. It opened a whole new world to her and her daily swim gives her great pleasure.

We're not saying changing an attitude about a gift that disappoints always works. There's no way Susan can live with that gaudy, heroic eagle painted on velvet Dan thought "interesting."

## One Last Thought on Disappointments

You might want to ask, is it really worth being disappointed about? All gifts do not have the same impact or carry the same importance. Learn to evaluate. Mellowing out and lightening up, as a wise woman once told us, is not a bad way to go sometimes. Or, maybe it's time to be creative about letting him know what pleases you. One woman told us it depends on how often you feel disappointed. If you respond without much enthusiasm to each of his gifts after he has really tried to please you, you will indeed discourage him. Can he handle one more, "If you'd just do it better"? You may need to reread "Thanks, I Think" our chapter on responding to gifts. "Some women are just too finicky," one relaxed grandmother told us.

**In Summary** Having brooded over several disappointing gifts along our long paths, we decided brooding is not the way to go. Maybe it's time to be creative about letting him know what pleases you.

# 26: How to Tell Him What You Want

*Be obscure clearly.*
*E.B. White*

---

We know it is hard for some people, men and women, to ask for things; and if you have never done it, you will feel a bit strange.

We know that many of you feel you drop hints all over the place, so you can't understand how he can not know what to get you.

We also know that some of you have men in your lives who ask you what you would like, and you give that same worn out answer, "Oh, anything will be fine."

If you are just learning how to ask yourself or in a new relationship, there are some things to keep in mind. First of all, it is a good idea to ask him how he would like to handle gift selection for you. How would he like you to let him know? Ask him! That may settle the whole issue if he says he would like a list. And until you see how well he choose to match your taste, you have a way to communicate.

It gets a bit more complicated if he says he likes to figure things out for himself. Then you need to make sure your hints are not too vague or too scattershot. He could miss them. Dropping successful hints is truly an art. Leaving circled ads, thoroughly describing something you liked, getting friends to make suggestions — all of these are definite possibilities.

Advanced hinting can go as far as this suggestion from Dear Abby to a disappointed woman who wanted a better Valentine's Day

> DEAR ABBY: Another St. Valentine's Day has come and gone without flowers, candy or any kind of a valentine from my husband.
>
> I'm 25 and he is 26, and we've been married for three years. I'd have been thrilled if he had brought me a flower — or even handed me a valentine — but he ignored the day completely.
>
> Abby, the newspapers were filled with ads for gifts, and the store windows were decorated with hearts and flowers to remind people of that special day for lovers.
>
> He's a super guy, hardworking and decent, so maybe I shouldn't complain. But it sure would have felt great to have been remembered on St. Valentine's Day. Any ideas?
>
> NOBODY'S VALENTINE
>
> **Dear Nobody's: So another St. Valentine's Day has come and gone. You were forgotten, and now you're hurt.**
>
> **Well, don't let it happen again. A Week before St. Valentine's Day, leave a note on his pillow. "Only six more days before St. Valentine's Day — start shopping for a card."**
>
> **The following day, tape a note on the bathroom mirror, "Only five more days ...a single rose would be nice." The next day, stick an artificial flower in his shoe with another reminder. I think you get the idea.**
>
> **Some men need more reminding than others, so don't sit silently with your fingers crossed,**

**hoping he'll remember. Some good-humored "reminding" can save you the pain of being forgotten.**

**And he may even appreciate it.**

Would such an overt action be hard for you? It is not so easy for many women to fully realize that they must take some action if they are unhappy with the gift situation as it exists. He needs you to tell him what you really want. This allows him to get some pleasure too, he gets to feel good about his actions.

For the third woman we mentioned. You are not really helping him with vague, open-ended responses. Remember, no myths here. He is busy and caring; help him out — get creative. It does not have to be expensive — time alone or with him could be your dream come true.

**What else can you do?**

Nothing beats open, honest and gentle communication. Give him this book to read. Then sit down together and review the ideas. Let him know what gifts please you the most. Be specific. This is a chance to get the message straight. This is NOT the time to tell him what he has done poorly in the past. Positive approach only here.

Listen to his side of the gift giving dilemma and how it can often be a problem for him. Correct old undesirable patterns as soon as possible so they don't get repeated.

And choose a time to do this when you both are relaxed and have some time to be together.

# 27: Gifting Yourself

This is for you who have

1) **read every word and tried every idea about how to appreciate gifts,**

2) **left him enough hints, ideas and suggestions to fill a two pound catalogue,**

3) **tried every imaginative thing in your head to get his attention.**

Still, he just doesn't get it, or he's out of town, or he has the memory span of a gnat.

Whatever his good points, he's a total washout in the gift department. That means it's time to take charge. It's time to do-it-yourself. As the *Wall Street Journal*[19] says, "It's time for Self-Basting."

"It ought to be easy to give myself a present. I treat myself everyday." No, No, — go back two spaces. You're missing the best part. Remember the **Do It Right.** What is it you wish he'd have sent you? A single red rose? (Wrap it beautifully — include a crystal or silver vase.) A dozen pink carnations, like the ones you saw together in Paris? (Have them tied with pink silk ribbons). For jewelry, pick something you really like, (have it engraved, have the jeweler send it special delivery). If you choose it far enough ahead it may even be a surprise when you open it.

The *Spiegel Catalogue* ran an ad last year illustrating this concept:

> Once upon a Christmas, Jamee dreamed of a special doll, one that is incredibly life-like and dressed in pretty clothing. She wished with all her might that it would be waiting for her under the tree. Alas, Jamee's wish wasn't answered — because her husband thought she was too old to play with dolls. But one doesn't play with the most beautiful dolls in the whole world; one admires them like fine crystal. So Jamee took out her charge card and ordered a Madame Alexander doll for herself. And she lived happily ever after.

Jane had hinted on many occasions to her husband that she would love a big celebration on her birthday. In the past it hadn't happened and she was often disappointed. Although ordinarily a very considerate man, he was no winner in the gifting department. So, at age 35, she decided to make arrangements for her own birthday party. And it was a good thing she did. On the eve of the party he was called out of town on business. The party went on as planned and later he told her how relieved and pleased he was that she would be happy on her birthday. He even sent her a dozen red roses.

There's another aspect of gifting yourself which has nothing to do with your spouse. In other parts of the world there are other customs. Birthdays in some countries like the Netherlands are for bringing together the people you want most to see. The Birthday Person has an open house and guests drop by all day. Any version of this custom can be great fun and a great way to gift yourself.

**Observation:** Gifting Yourself in just the way you'd like it is a good alternative for women whose spouses don't or can't participate in the gift process. Above all, make the gift to yourself frivolous, make it extravagant, have fun with it. And congratulate yourself on your ability to solve this gift giving problem for yourself.

# References

**THE GIFT PROBLEM**

1. Cowherd, Kevin. "Secrets of Buying Gifts for a Woman," *San Francisco Chronicle* (April 17, 1989.)

**UNRAVELING THE MYSTERY**

2. Masello, Robert. "What Guys Don't Get About Gift Giving," *Mademoiselle,* (July, 1984), p.92.

3. Jacoby, Susan. "The Hidden Message in Your Gift," *McCall's,* (January, 1983), p.8.

4. Bryan, Dawn. *The Art And Etiquette of Gift Giving.* New York: Bantam, 1987.

5. Broyard, Anatole. "With Each Gift a Message," *House Beautiful*, December, 1983, p. 50.

**MORE OF WHAT MEN TOLD US**

6. Ibid., Broyard.

7. Stern, Barbara Lange. "Gifts' Meanings and Why You May Feel Uneasy About Accepting Them," *Vogue,* Vol. 176 (June, 1986), p. 296.

**FEAR OF SHOPPING**

8. "Great Expectations," *Esquire,* June 19, 1990.

**HOW TO FIND OUT WHAT SHE WANTS**

9. Ibid.

**WHAT TYPE IS SHE?**

10. Scanlon, Susan. *Type Reporter*, Vol. 3 No. 7 (December, 1988.)

11. Scanlon, Susan. *Type Reporter*, Vol. 4 No. 5 (October, 1989.)

**BUYING HER JEWELRY**

12. Graham, Ellen. "A Holiday Hint," *Wall Street Journal*, (December 9, 1990.)

**BUYING HER FLOWERS**

13. *Marin Independent Journal*. (February 12, 1989.)

**TO CATALOGUE OR NOT**

14. *Consumer Reports*, (October, 1987), p.607.

**IT'S ALL IN THE DELIVERY**

15. Masello, op.cit.

**PUTTING IT IN WRITING**

16. Shapiro, Brenda. "Between Friends and Lovers," *Chicago*.

**VALENTINE'S DAY**

17. Waggoner, Glen and Moloney, Kathleen. *Esquire Etiquette: The Modern Man's Guide to Good Form*. New York: MacMillan, 1987.

**STATES OF ROMANCE**

18. "California Romance, Where to Find It", *WW*, (April 4-11, 1988.)

**ONE SURVEY SAYS**

19. Loc. cit., *Esquire*.

**HOW TO TELL HIM WHAT YOU WANT**

20. Dear Abby. *San Francisco Chronicle*, (February 12, 1990.)

**GIFTING YOURSELF**

21. Loc. cit., *Wall Street Journal*.

## ABOUT THE AUTHORS

Georgia and Rita have worked together on many projects. Their previous co-authored book was *The Balanced Woman.*

For the past fifteen years Georgia has been co-director of Cable Car Seminar and Tours, a convention service company in San Francisco. Prior to that she was the director of continuing education for women a Foothill College for which she received numerous programming awards. Of great importance to her are her husband and three grown children.

Rita currently works as a management development consultant and has been a marriage counselor for twelve years in the San Francisco area. She lives with her husband Jerry and occasionally with her two sons who move in and out. Her two cats are more stationary.

## REORDER FORM

If you would like your friends to have their own personal copy of GIFT GIVING *From Him to Her* please send a check or money order for $10.95 Plus 7 1/2% to cover California taxes, plus shipping.

Shipping: Book Rate- $1.75 for first book and $0.75 for each additional book. (Surface shipping may take three to four weeks.) Air Mail - $3.00 per book

Mail to:

Sunkist House
196 Sunkist Lane
Los Altos, CA 94022

Please make checks payable to Sunkist House Publishing

I am enclosing $_____ for _____ books.

Please send GIFT GIVING to:

Name

_____

Address_____

_____